LEONARDO'S
ART
WORKSHOP

Brimming with creative inspiration, how-to projects, and useful information to enrich your everyday life, Quarto Knows is a favorite destination for those pursuing their interests and passions. Visit our site and dig deeper with our books into your area of interest: Quarto Creates, Quarto Cooks, Quarto Homes, Quarto Lives, Quarto Drives, Quarto Explores, Quarto Gifts, or Quarto Kids.

First published in 2019 by Rockport Publishers, an imprint of The Quarto Group, 100 Cummings Center, Suite 265-D, Beverly, MA 01915, USA.
T (978) 282-9590 F (978) 283-2742
QuartoKnows.com

Rockport Publishers titles are also available at discount for retail, wholesale, promotional, and bulk purchase. For details, contact the Special Sales Manager by email at specialsales@quarto.com or by mail at The Quarto Group, Attn: Special Sales Manager, 401 Second Avenue North, Suite 310, Minneapolis, MN 55501, USA.

10 9 8 7 6 5 4 3 2 1

ISBN: 978-1-63159-522-6

Digital edition published in 2018
eISBN: 978-1-63159-523-3

Library of Congress Cataloging-in-Publication Data

Leidtke, Amy, author.
Leonardo's art workshop : invent, create, and make STEAM projects like
  a genius / Amy Leidtke.
ISBN 9781631595233 (e-book) | ISBN 9781631595226 (pbk.)
1. Art--Technique--Juvenile literature. 2. Visual
  perception--Juvenile literature. 3. Leonardo,
  da Vinci, 1452-1519--Knowledge and learning--
  Juvenile literature. 4. Science--Study and
  teaching (Elementary)--Activity programs.
LCC N7430.5 (ebook)
LCC N7430.5 .L437 2019 (print)
  702.8--dc23
2018021601 (print)
2 018021958 (ebook)

Design and layout: Burge Agency
Cover image: Glenn Scott Photography

Photography: Amy Leidtke; except pages 19–21, 30–31, 37–39, 54–55, Glenn Scott Photography; Shutterstock (credits on page 139); and Bridgeman Images (credits on page 138).
Illustration: Amy Leidtke

Printed in China

LEONARDO'S

ArT WORKSHOP

INVENT, CREATE,
AND MAKE **STEAM**
PROJECTS LIKE
A GENIUS

ROCKPORT

AMY LEIDTKE

This is a model of Leonardo's design for what he called an aerial screw (helicopter). He was fascinated with the idea of human flight and might have designed this flying machine for an elaborate pageant or theatrical performance—another pursuit that he enjoyed.

CONTENTS

INTRODUCTION 6
EVERYTHING IS CONNECTED

CHAPTER 1 9
COLOR

The Science of Color 10
Rainbow Science 16
Transparent Color 22
Color in Art and Light 28
The Visual Language of Color 32

CHAPTER 2 35
SHADOW AND LIGHT

The Nature of Light 36
Light and the Eye 40
The Nature of Shadows 46
Chiaroscuro Drawing 52
Five O'Clock Shadow 56

CHAPTER 3 61
LINES AND PATTERNS

Following the Line 62
Lines that Define 68
Lines that Aren't There 73
Lines that Jump Off the Page 78

CHAPTER 4 85
FORMS AND STRUCTURES

The Mathematics of Art 86
The Geometry of Art 92
The Geometry of Architecture 98
Playing with Form 104

CHAPTER 5 113
OPTICS AND SPECIAL EFFECTS

The Eye and Perception 114
The Illusion of Motion 118
Art Mirrors Life 122
The Eye Mixes Color 126

CHAPTER 6 131
THE ESSENTIAL LEONARDO

DIY Leonardo Notebook: Make a notebook and use it—like a genius! 136

Photo Credits 138
Resources 140
About the Author 141
Acknowledgments 141
Index 142

EVERYTHING IS CONNECTED

Sometimes, things that don't seem to start out well turn out to be the best things after all. Leonardo had a very humble start when he was born in the small town of Vinci, in Tuscany, Italy, in 1452. His father, Piero, a well-off legal notary, didn't marry Leonardo's mother, a peasant named Caterina. Not only was Leonardo not expected to follow in his father's footsteps and become a notary, but that kind of education and career were not available to him.

In fact, he would have very little formal education at all. But he got something better for a boy full of curiosity. By the time he was fourteen, Leonardo's talent as an artist was already evident, and his father found him a position as an apprentice, working in the studio of the painter and sculptor Andrea del Verrocchio in the great city of Florence.

Leonardo didn't often get to show his love of animals in his paintings, but he did in this portrait of Cecilia Gallerani, *The Lady with the Ermine*, 1496.

The hill town of Vinci where Leonardo was born.

Florence during the Renaissance was *the* place for exchanging ideas about art, architecture, and engineering. Artists and writers—all the creative minds of the city—stopped by Verrocchio's studio to look, talk about art, exchange news, and discuss ideas. Young Leonardo could listen in and, in time, take part in those discussions, getting to know all the great thinkers of the day. It was the perfect place for his genius as an artist and inventor to blossom and his education to begin.

For Leonardo, everything was connected. Art wasn't just about applying paint with a brush. In studying painting, he studied the landscape. In studying the landscape, he taught himself about perspective—how things seem to disappear in the distance, a form of mathematics that allows an artist to create a three-dimensional scene on a flat painting surface. By studying weather and rivers, he taught himself about wind and water flow, buoyancy, gravity, and energy—in other words, physics. In studying the life cycle of trees, he pioneered new ideas about ecological systems. And in studying rocks, he learned about geology and how the Earth was formed. Leonardo included depictions of rivers and rock formations in many of his paintings, and they are so true to the originals that geologists looking at them today can identify each kind of rock.

The art historian Kenneth Clark called Leonardo "the most relentlessly curious man in history," and that just might be true. He was fascinated by nature, he loved knowing not just how things work but why they work, and he loved the world. He was curious about everything in it. For Leonardo, to study and understand one subject meant comparing it with all the other subjects that he had investigated. And as his learning advanced in one field, he adjusted his notes and conclusions in the other fields as well.

He began his studies as a painter, but during his long life, Leonardo's curiosity, diligence, and genius made him a master painter, sculptor, architect, designer, scientist, engineer, and inventor. There was no separation between art, science, and mathematics in his mind. Does this sound like STEAM? You bet it does. More than 500 years ago, Leonardo knew that the fields of science, technology, engineering, art, and mathematics (STEAM) are all connected, and on the pages of this book, we'll help you, too, to see how art, math, and science are all connected.

On these pages from one of Leonardo's notebooks, he sketched clouds, plants, a rearing horse, a man in profile, engineering ideas, and more—proof of a curious and wide-ranging mind on a single spread of a notebook.

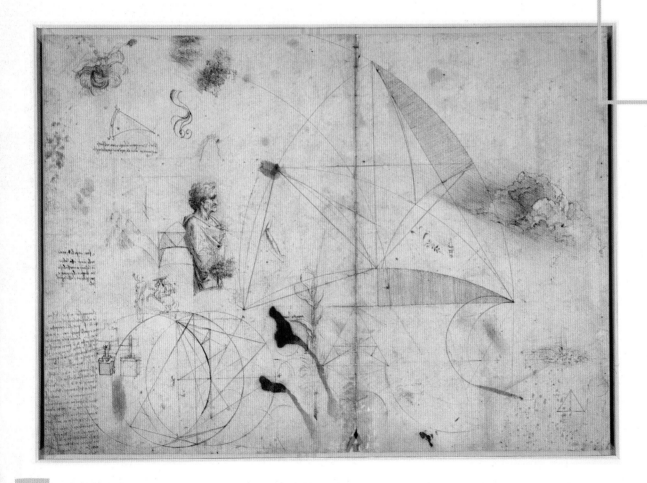

CHAPTER 1

COLOR

THE SCIENCE OF COLOR

Why do we see different colors, and where do they come from?

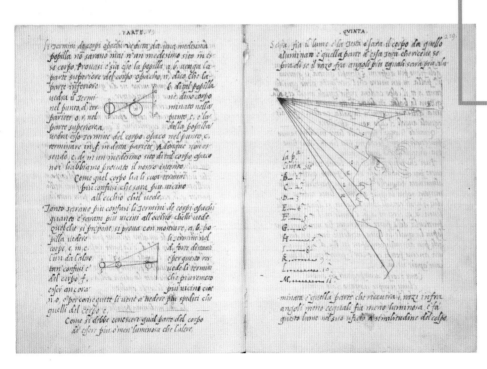

Leonardo recorded notes on his studies of light rays throughout his notebooks.

Leonardo looked at everything he did from every possible angle. As a painter, he studied the geometry of light rays and the nature of shadows. As an artist's apprentice in the 1460s, he learned to grind glass lenses and was fascinated with using them to focus light, which he recognized as a form of energy. Later, he also experimented with refraction (bending light by passing it through a prism) and watched the magical results. He wrote about his experiments in his notebooks, but he never published his results. Credit for the discovery of the color in light would go to another scientist, Sir Isaac Newton in England, who published his own studies some 200 years later.

There are light waves all around, but the only ones humans can see are those in the visible spectrum. The full spectrum of light waves includes infrared rays, visible light, ultraviolet rays, and X-rays. Human eyes are only sensitive to the range of wavelengths between 780 and 380 nanometers—our visible spectrum. There may be far more colors that we can't see. Ultraviolet, for instance, is invisible to our eyes, but bees can see it, and they use it to detect nectar.

How long is a nanometer?

Nanometer (abbreviation nm) means "dwarf meter." It's a metric unit of length equal to one-billionth of a meter (0.000000001 m). Try measuring that with a ruler!

VISIBLE AND INVISIBLE LIGHT

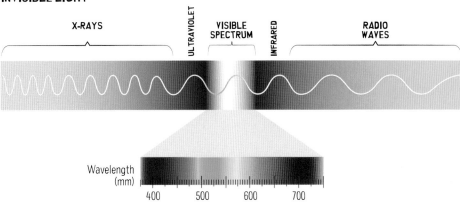

VISIBLE LIGHT

In experimenting with prisms in the 1670s, Sir Isaac made the same discovery that Leonardo had. He discovered the secret of color: Sunlight passing through a prism produces a rainbow when it falls onto a surface because light from the sun, called white light, contains the color spectrum.

Sunlight is radiant energy, and, like other forms of energy, it travels in wavelengths. We see different wavelengths of visible light as different colors. We call the spectrum that we're familiar with the visible spectrum.

ARE BLACK AND WHITE COLORS?

Leonardo wrote about the question of black and white as colors in his *Treatise on Painting.* Even at the time he wrote it, in the late fifteenth century, he understood that artists considered black and white as colors because they needed to *use* them as colors. But to a scientist (or a philosopher in Leonardo's day), black and white are not colors—and not only because they don't appear in the spectrum.

Black is the absence of visible light, and so it has no color. That's easy to understand since color comes from light—cut off all sources of light, and the room goes completely dark. But white contains all the wavelengths of visible light and is the combination of all colors, and that's harder to understand. As you already know, if you try mixing all the colors in a pan of watercolors together, you don't get white. So how does that work?

Sir Isaac Newton experimented with prisms, but he also experimented with color wheels. In fact, he invented the color wheel. First, he divided white sunlight into a spectrum of red, orange, yellow, green, cyan, and blue beams. Then, he joined the two ends of the spectrum together to make a circle, or wheel, with the progression of colors going around it. When he spun the wheel, something interesting happened. (See the project on the next page.)

This is a replica of Newton's color wheel.

DISAPPEARING COLOR

NEWTON'S COLOR WHEEL

What happens when we spin a color wheel? Spinning a wheel of the colors of the rainbow turns it into white. Why? By spinning the disc of colors, we mix all of the different wavelengths of color together, turning them back into white light. Try it: Make color disappear and solve the mystery of how white can be a combination of all colors.

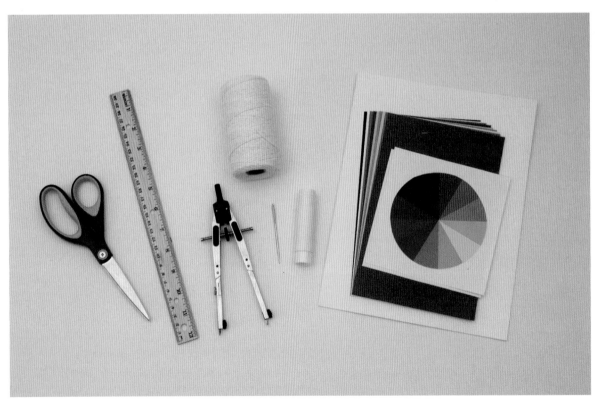

WHAT YOU WILL NEED

Color photocopier

Heavy white cardstock

Scissors

Pencil

Glue stick

Large upholstery needle or awl

Two 24" (61 cm) pieces of string

Colored cardstock (optional)

Drawing compass (optional)

1 Make two color copies of this color wheel on white cardstock. Print at 100% (4 1/2" or 11.4 cm)

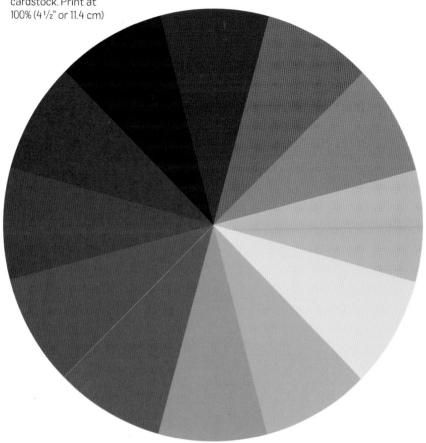

2 Cut out the two wheels.

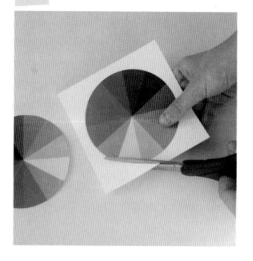

3 Use the glue stick to attach the cutout color wheels back to back. Be sure to use plenty of glue so the color discs don't come loose when they spin

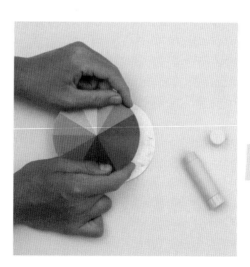

4 Use the needle to poke two small holes, about 1/2" (1.3 cm) apart, through the center of the wheels.

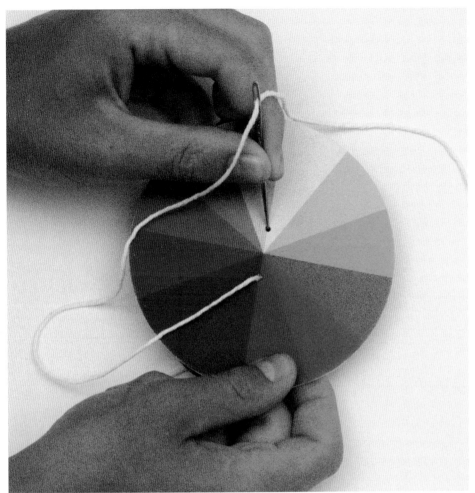

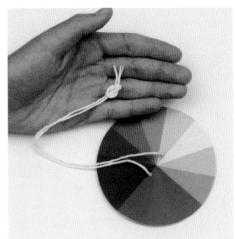

5 Thread one piece of string through the hole of the needle. Thread the needle through the holes.

6 Tie the ends of the string together, forming a loop. You've made a string handle for one side of the disc. Repeat steps 5 and 6 to form a string handle for the opposite side.

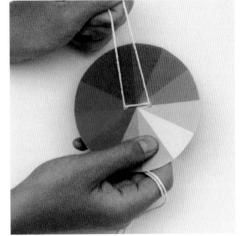

7 Pull the string handles so that the disc is centered.

8 Holding the string handles by the ends, wind the disc by spinning it away from you—like turning a jump rope.

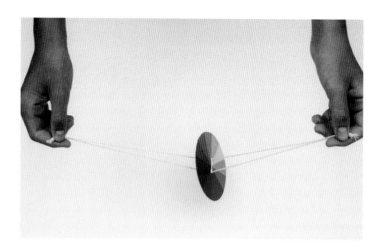

Try more color-wheel experiments with collaged color. Cut colorful bits of paper and glue them to a paper disc. What happens if you limit your palette—say, using only red and yellow—and spin the disc? Can you combine colors to make other colors appear? Try slowing down the spin. Does the speed at which your disc spins make a difference in what you see?

9 Continue until the disc is tightly wound (the twisted strings will double up).

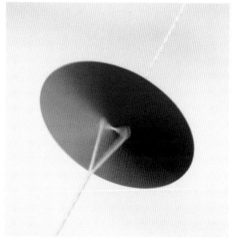

10 Gently pull the string outward on both sides at the same time. The disc will spin fast—watch what happens as the spinning colors merge.

A rainbow over the mountains of Italy.

RAINBOW SCIENCE

When sunlight passes through an ordinary pane of window glass, it appears simply as white light. But when sunlight passes through a prism, the colors of the spectrum appear. How does that happen?

HOW PRISMS WORK: THE MAGIC OF REFRACTION

In **geometry**, a prism is a solid form with identical ends and flat sides. The end shape gives the prism a name, like *square prism* or *triangular prism*. All of the sides are parallelograms.

In **optics**, a prism is a transparent, polished glass or plastic form. The most common prism form is a triangular prism.

Scientists and artists use prisms for their ability to bend, or refract, light. It's the way the side surfaces face each other in the prism that allows it to do this; light enters one side of the prism and then refracts and is slowed down, changing direction as it passes out the other side.

When the light bends, something magical happens: the colors that are already in the light also bend, and they spread out, depending on their individual wavelengths, in a process called dispersion. When they pass through the prism and land on a wall or other surface, you see them as their beautiful color spectrum.

WHY DO RAINBOWS APPEAR?

Rainbows are as fascinating as they are beautiful. You can be walking down the road on a misty gray day and turn the corner, and suddenly you're looking at one of nature's greatest color creations. But then, even as you watch, it disappears.

Rainbows only occur when there is exactly the right combination of sun and rain. In order for you to see one, the sun must be behind you, and there must be rain or mist ahead of you. You have the best chance of seeing a rainbow on an afternoon when the rain showers are moving from west to east. (The sun will be at your back in the west in the afternoon, and the rainbow will appear in the east.)

The raindrops in the air act as miniature versions of the prisms you've just read about. Sunlight shines onto a raindrop, bounces off the curved back of the raindrop, and is reflected into your eyes. The light refracts again as it passes through the raindrop—or mini prism—and disperses as a colorful spectrum.

THE END OF THE RAINBOW

You've probably heard the saying that there's a pot of gold at the end of the rainbow. Because rainbows are so magical, people have associated them with all sorts of things like good luck and happy endings. But in reality, there is no end of the rainbow!

The arc that we see when we look at rainbows from Earth is actually part of a circle—a true color wheel. Full-circle rainbows have a special name—they're called "the glory," and the glory can only be seen from the sky. (When we look at a rainbow from Earth, the horizon line cuts the full circle from our vision.) Not many people have had the good luck to see the glory. Look for one the next time you fly.

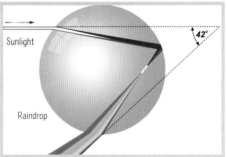

RAINBOW MATH

You don't see rainbows every time the sun comes out when it rains. Why not? Because a rainbow is only visible when sunlight strikes raindrops at a shallow angle, around 42 degrees, causing it to be refracted and then dispersed back toward the viewer. Less than 42 degrees and the light will just pass through the bottom of the raindrop; wider than 42 degrees and the light will reflect back out through the top.

DID YOU KNOW?

The rainbow you see belongs to you. The rainbow you see depends on the light hitting the raindrops directly in your line of vision. Someone standing near you will also see a rainbow, but because they'll be seeing it through a different set of raindrops, they'll be seeing a different rainbow!

BUT WAIT! THERE'S AN EXCEPTION

There is one exception to the rain-plus-sunshine rule for rainbows. Sometimes a little moonglow will do: The result is a moonbow. Moonbows are made in exactly the same way as a rainbow, when the moon's light is reflected and refracted off raindrops in the air. Hold on a second! Does the moon give off light? Well, no, but the sun does. The light we see on the moon is actually reflected from the sun. We say "moon's light" as a poetic way to express this idea.

COLOR SCIENCE

Meet ROY G BIV. Who? These letters stand for the colors of the spectrum: Red, Orange, Yellow, Green, Blue, Indigo, Violet. "ROY G BIV" is just an easy way to remember them.

Whether you look at a rainbow produced from a prism, one you create with a garden hose, or one in the sky, the colors always fall in exactly the same order—red on top, violet at the bottom. Why? The answer lies in wavelengths.

A single color is represented by a single wavelength, and each color has its own wavelength, different from all the others. Red wavelengths are the longest, around 780 to 622 nanometers (see page 11). They are followed by orange at 622 to 597 nanometers, yellow at 597 to 577 nanometers, green at 577 to 492 nanometers, blue at 492 to 455 nanometers. Last in the list is violet, whose waves are the shortest at 455 to 390 nanometers. The wavelengths fall in descending order, and—*voilà!*—so do the colors.

 BUT WAIT! THERE'S AN EXCEPTION
There is an exception to the red-on-top rule, and you can see it in the sky on those rare occasions when there is a double rainbow. As you can see in this picture, the second, fainter rainbow has the colors reversed. So how does that happen?

For the primary (brighter) rainbow, the light only has to reflect off each raindrop once before refracting out of the raindrop.

The secondary rainbow occurs when the refracted light reflects off the raindrop's surface *a second time*. This means that it creates a reflection of the primary rainbow. And, as you know, when you look at a reflection, everything is reversed! In this case, that means violet on top, red on the bottom.

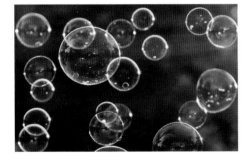

WHY DO WE SEE BRILLIANT RAINBOW COLORS ON BUBBLES?
Sometimes we see marvelous patterns of colors, or iridescence, on soap bubbles. The walls of bubbles actually consist of a thin layer of water sandwiched between two thin layers of soap. The amount of iridescence depends on the varying thickness (unevenness) of the bubble wall. We can't perceive any differences in the thickness of a bubble wall with our eyes, but a wave of light can tell the difference.

Because bubbles are transparent, light reflects on both their outer and inner surfaces. Each change of distance matches the wavelength of a specific color of light, so the colors change, or iridesce, with the size of a bubble and the thickness of its walls.

HARNESS A RAINBOW

In this project, you'll discover how changing the size of an aperture (opening) that lets light in can change what you see. Experiment with making rainbows of different lengths, different shapes, and different sizes. All you need is a darkened room and a few simple tools, including a flashlight*, some cardstock, and a prism.

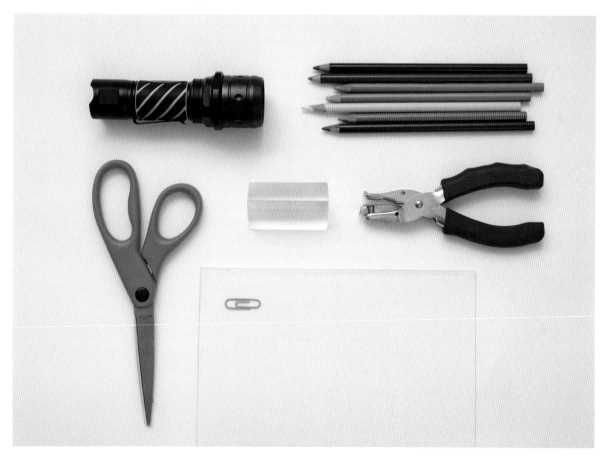

WHAT YOU WILL NEED

Four sheets 8½" × 11" (21.5 × 28 cm) cardstock

Scissors

Hole punch

Paperclip

Triangular prism

Masking tape

30" (76 cm) string

Flashlight (not LED)

Colored pencils (red, orange, yellow, green, blue, indigo, and violet)

*Note: To work with the prism, you'll need a flashlight with a bulb light, *not* an LED light.

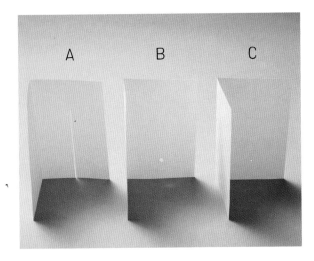

1 Fold three of the sheets of cardstock in half widthwise so they can stand up on their own.

2 Create a different aperture in each sheet:
A. Use the scissors to cut a thin slit in the first. The slit should be less than ⅛" (3 mm) wide and taller than the height of the prism.
B. Use the hole punch to make a hole in the second sheet.
C. Use the paperclip to make a hole in the third.

3 Choose one of the apertures. Line up the prism, aperture, and flashlight.

4 Darken the room and turn on the flashlight. Aim the beam through the aperture and onto the prism. Observe what happens when you change the position of the flashlight. Do the shapes of the rainbows change depending on how you hold the flashlight? Does the spectrum change in size when you alter the position of the prism?

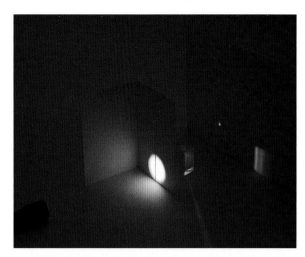

5 Record the spectrum using color pencils and the fourth sheet of cardstock.

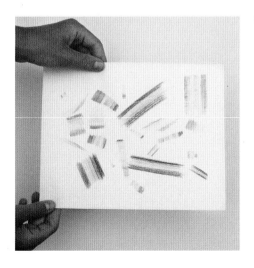

6 Repeat steps 3 to 5, using the other two apertures. Fill the sheet with all the rainbows you captured.

TAKE IT FURTHER

Can you make the rainbow move around the room? What if you hang the prism and shine light on it from different angles? For this experiment, tape a piece of string to a prism and suspend it in the air. You might need an extra set of hands!

Take it even further: What if you tried using a glass full of water as a prism? This time, make an aperture on the flashlight by using tape to cover all but a slit opening on the face of the flashlight. Place the water on the edge of a table. Put the cardstock on the floor. Darken the room. Aim the flashlight through the water. Adjust the position and angle of the flashlight to observe how the rainbow changes. Record the rainbow—try using a camera to photograph it.

To add rainbows to a room, place a prism near a window on a sunny day.

TRANSPARENT COLOR

Our visible spectrum comes to us as seven beautiful transparent colors, but when they're mixed, hundreds (maybe endless!) more colors can be created. Sometimes nature does it for us—in the colors of light layering one over another in a magnificent sunset, for instance. Sometimes we do it ourselves—like when we create film, digital imagery, printed paper, dyed fabrics, or even icing for cakes.

"WHEN A TRANSPARENT COLOR IS LAID DOWN UPON ANOTHER OF A DIFFERENT NATURE, IT PRODUCES A MIXED COLOR, DIFFERENT FROM EITHER OF THE SIMPLE ONES THAT COMPOSE IT."
—Leonardo, from his *Treatise on Painting*

A PAINTING BREAKTHROUGH

Until Leonardo's day, when artists created a portrait for an important person or a major painting for a church, they worked with egg tempera. This beautiful medium is made by mixing finely ground pigments with egg yolk and small amounts of water. Egg tempera dries very quickly and is nearly opaque when it dries, which makes blending colors difficult.

A revolution in painting took place in the fifteenth century, when a new type of paint—oil paint—was widely adopted by artists. Leonardo was one of the first to master the medium. For this new type of paint, artists mixed their ground pigments with an oil, such as linseed oil, which dries slowly. Oil paint can be applied in very thin coats of *transparent* color, which allows the color underneath it to show through.

Leonardo discovered that in laying down thin layers of color, one on top of another, he could blend and model them, creating luminous depths of color in shadows, skin tones, fabrics, hair, and even a person's eyes. You can see the effect in this portrait that he painted of an angel.

Transparent oils allowed Leonardo to create the illusion that light is coming from within the painting. It also allowed him to master painting a realistic atmosphere and range of tones in a landscape. Some say his mastery of color technique has never been surpassed. In his usual way, Leonardo did not simply make use of the new medium, he explored everything that could be done with it.

Leonardo's face of an angel. Detail from *Virgin of the Rocks*, 1483-1490.

Powdered pigment for sale at a market stall for artists.

WHERE DO PIGMENTS COME FROM?

Oil paint didn't come in a tube in Leonardo's day. Artists made their own paint, mixing linseed or walnut oil with ground pigments. But where did the pigments come from? Suppliers of art materials looked everywhere and at everything, from plants and insects in the garden to rocks and clay deep in the earth, to find useable color. They even imported semiprecious stones, bringing in lapis lazuli, for example, all the way from Afghanistan because it was bright blue—one of the more difficult pigments to find in nature. Some pigments, such as arsenic, which produces orange, were poisonous! Art was a treasure hunt even before the painting began.

CREATE PAINT AND DYES FROM FOOD

Color occurs naturally in plants. Organic pigments called carotenoids in carrots, for instance, produce yellow, orange, and red; anthocyanins in beets and blueberries create red, purple, and blue; and chlorophyll in leafy plants such as spinach produces green. In this project, you'll use ground herbs and spices to make paint and the foods of your choice to make dye to color a piece of fabric or string.

Eggs colored with dyes from fruits and vegetables.

PROJECT 1: FOOD-BASED PAINT

Use water and common kitchen-cupboard ingredients to make translucent (semitransparent) paint similar to oil paint. These pigments will make colors similar to Naples Yellow, Yellow Ochre, Raw Sienna, Burnt Sienna, Venetian Red, and Raw Umber used by artists.

WHAT YOU WILL NEED

Measuring spoons

½ teaspoon pigment (such as ground mustard, ginger, turmeric, paprika, cinnamon, or unsweetened cocoa)

½ teaspoon water

Small microwavable bowl

Spoon

½ teaspoon honey

Paintbrushes

Several sheets 8½" × 11" (21.5 × 28 cm) white cardstock

1 Combine the pigment and water in the small bowl.

2 Mix the pigment and water with a spoon to create a thick paste.

3 Add the honey, which will act as a binder.

4 Mix well and heat in a microwave for 10 to 15 seconds. Repeat if needed. Why heat? It causes the plant-based pigment to break down, releasing color (and aroma).

5 Mix again, and—*voilà!*—you've made paint.

6 Using a brush, test the paint on the cardstock. If it's too thin, add more pigment. If it's too thick, thin it by adding a little bit of water. If you want to make the paint more like a translucent glaze, add a smidge more honey.

7 Once the consistency is just right, try creating a painting. Resist touching it—it should be dry by the next day.

PROJECT 2: FOOD-BASED DYES

Warning: Do not taste these dyes!

In this project, you will extract natural dye from plants. In the chart below, you'll see that, for some dyes, only a specific part of a vegetable or berry is used, while for others it's the whole thing. A mash of whole blueberries is used for purple dye, for instance, but only the skins of onions are used for yellow dye. Save the onion skins next time you make onion soup! Onion skins are dry, and you can put them aside and save them until you have enough for a bath of dye.

In this example, we are making purple dye with blueberries, but feel free to follow along using any column you'd like. The method is always the same.

WHAT YOU WILL NEED

6 ounces (170 g) of the vegetable or berry of your choice from row 2 in the chart below

Large pot

Long spoon for stirring

Measuring spoons

Measuring cups

3 teaspoons (15 ml) alum (used for pickling)

1½ teaspoons (7.5 ml) cream of tartar

1 quart (0.95 liter) water

White cotton cloth or string* that is thoroughly wet (dunk it in water, wring it, and repeat)

Tongs

Rubber gloves

*It's important that the cloth or string be cotton and not a synthetic material. Synthetics will not absorb color easily.

	PURPLE	LIGHT YELLOW	ORANGE	MAGENTA	DARK GREEN
Plant	Blueberry	Onion	Carrot	Beets	Spinach
Part of plant to use	Berries	Skins	Roots	Roots	Leaves
What to do to the plant before using	Mash the berries	Pound the onion skins	Shred the carrot roots	Shred the beet roots	Cut the spinach leaves
Plant pigment	Anthocyanin	Cepaic acid	Carotene	Betanin	Chlorophyll

TO MAKE THE DYE:

1   Prepare the plant according to row 3 in the chart. Put it in a large cooking pot.

2   Add the water to the pot and heat it to the point of simmering. Let it simmer for up to an hour.

4   Pull on the rubber gloves and use the tongs to carefully remove the cloth or string from the dye. Place it in the sink under cool running water to rinse away the remaining bits of food pigment. The water will also rinse away the excess dye. Rinse until the water runs clear—a minute or two.

5   Squeeze (or press) the cloth or string to remove the excess water. Hang it to dry. Be sure to wash your hands with soap and water.

TO DYE THE CLOTH OR STRING:

1   Add the alum and cream of tartar to the dye and stir until combined.

2   Add the presoaked cloth or string. Stir until the dye soaks the material.

3   Simmer until the cloth or string is dyed. (At least 1 hour). The longer it simmers, the darker the color will be. Turn off the stove and allow the pot to cool.

TAKE IT FURTHER

If you want the color to last wash after wash, you will need to set (or lock) the dyed fabric in a special bath. In a clean, large bowl, combine 2 tablespoons (36 g) table salt, ½ cup (120 ml) vinegar, and 8 cups (1.9 L) water. Add the fabric to the bath and let it soak overnight before wringing out the excess liquid. Then dry the fabric.

TAKE IT EVER FURTHER

Use the string or cloth to make a project—a friendship bracelet or a customized dinner napkin, for instance.

COLOR IN ART AND LIGHT

RED, YELLOW, BLUE

As every artist knows, the three primary colors are red, blue, and yellow, which can be mixed to form the secondary colors of green, purple, and orange. In fact, if you have the three primary paint colors on your palette (and a little black and white on the side), you can play with combinations endlessly, changing the ratios to mix every color under the sun. And as you've probably discovered if you mix all three primary colors together, you get brown or a near black.

BUT WAIT! THERE'S AN EXCEPTION

When you're talking about mixing the colors of *light* instead of the colors of paint pigments, the three primary colors are not red, yellow, and blue but red, *green*, and blue. Light is pure color, while paint pigments (and everything else we look at around us) are *reflected* color. Pure color and pigments mix colors differently. With light, mixing every color under the sun begins with red, green, and blue.

WHAT DOES *REFLECTED* COLOR MEAN?

As you've already learned, color comes from light, and different colors in light travel at different wavelengths. Paint, pigments, fruits, flowers, and everything else we look at contain elements that absorb certain wavelengths of color and reflect others. A red flower, for instance, reflects only red and absorbs all the other colors in light. The color that reflects back to the receptors in our eyes is the color we see.

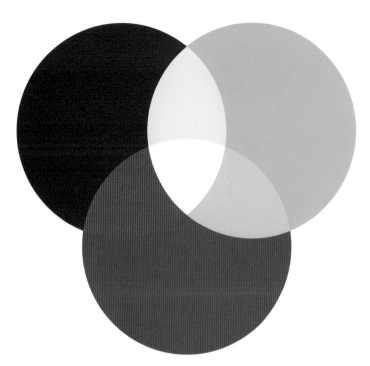

MIXING THE COLORS OF LIGHT

Artists who design theater lighting and decorate store-window displays work with color-light mixing all the time. But guess what? So do you every time you look at a computer or phone screen.

Computers don't use paint to create a beautiful picture for you—they use light instead. Mixing the colors of light is called *additive color*, and the colors you see when you look at the screen are all made by mixing red, green, and blue.

Look at what happens when the colors of light overlap to create secondary colors. Instead of the orange, green, and purple that you get when you mix paint pigments, you get magenta, yellow, and a light blue called cyan. Now look at the center of the diagram. When all three primary colors of light overlap, instead of turning into muddy brown or black as happens when you mix the primary colors of pigments, they return to white—the color of pure light from the sun.

MAGENTA, YELLOW, AND CYAN

Do these colors sound familiar? They might. If you ever change the toner in a color printer, you'll notice that magenta, yellow, and cyan are the names of the three color cartridges that, along with black, make all of the colors that you use for printing.

The *primary* colors of light (additive colors) are combined when you look at your computer screen, but the *secondary* colors of light combine when you print from your computer onto paper.

Look at what happens when magenta, yellow, and cyan overlap. They turn back into the primary colors of light: red, green, and blue! (Remember, this is because the pigment in your printer is *reflected* light.) Look again where all three colors overlap in the center— they turn into black, just as they do with the pigments in paint.

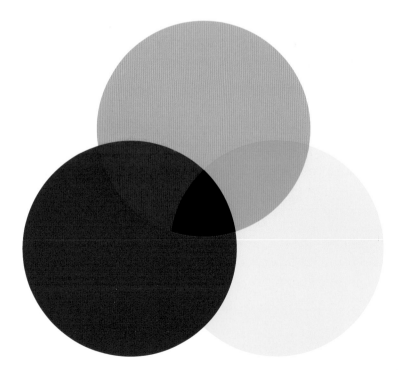

COLORFUL SHADOWS— RED, GREEN, BLUE

Explore mixing different colors of light to make colorful shadows.

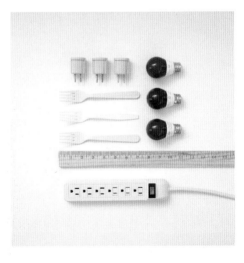

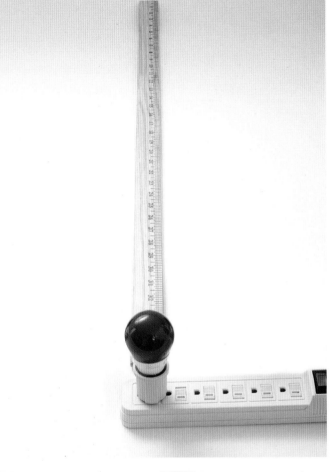

WHAT YOU WILL NEED

White wall or other large white surface

Thin objects (such as a pencil, spoon, fork, or scissors)

Three lightbulbs in red, green, and blue (compact fluorescent or LED)*

Three plug-in socket adapters*

Power strip

Measuring stick (yard stick or meter stick)

8½" × 11" (21.5 × 28 cm) sheet of white cardstock

*These items are available at hardware stores and online.

1 Arrange the equipment as shown here. Place the measuring stick perpendicular to the white wall and use it to measure the distance between the white surface and the bulbs. The bulbs should be at least 3 feet (0.9 m) away from the white surface.

2 Darken the room and turn on the red bulb. Line up the measuring stick with the red bulb.

TAKE IT FURTHER

Test 1: Focus all three lights on the same area of the white wall. What happens?

Test 2: Try moving the objects closer to the white wall. Try moving the light source closer to and then farther away from the white wall. Notice that the closer the object is to the wall, the smaller and sharper the shadow becomes.

Test 3: Cut a 1" (2.5 cm) hole in a white card. Hold it between the bulbs and the white wall. Compare different size holes and different shapes of holes, too.

What other tests can you think of? What happens if you shine the lights at a jar of colored water? Does the water cast its own light? What colors are its shadows? Try photographing your results.

3 Place a thin object on the measuring stick between the red bulb and the white wall, creating a shadow.

4 Repeat with each color. Notice how each color of light changes the color of the white wall and the shadow is always darker. Notice the shadow is lined up with the stick. This is because light rays travel in straight lines.

5 Turn on the green and red bulbs at the same time. Place another thin object between the red and green bulbs and the white wall. Notice how the color of the shadows and color of the white wall changes. How many shadows do you see? How many colors of shadows do you see? What colors are on the wall?

6 Turn on all three lights. Use another thin object to make shadows. How many shadows are there, and what color are they? If the lights are red, green, and blue, why are the shadows not the same?

THE VISUAL LANGUAGE OF COLOR

Stop signs in Arabic, Japanese, and English.

Close your eyes and try to imagine each of the following things. What color comes to mind as you do?

Touching something hot

Hearing a blaring car horn

Feeling angry

Feeling excited

Did you imagine red every time? How does that happen? Our minds make lightning-quick connections between colors and our senses and emotions. Red has many connections for us—all colors do. Are they the same for everyone? Let's find out.

WHAT DOES IT MEAN?

Every culture uses color to communicate ideas. But where do color meanings come from? Our interpretation of color is influenced by many things—where we live, what we believe, the people we hang out with, the music we listen to.

Sometimes, the meanings are practical: The color red is used in stop signs because it stands out.

Sometimes, the choices are seasonal: If you were decorating for a spring party, you probably would not use orange and gold because those colors make us think of autumn leaves and pumpkins.

Sometimes the colors are patriotic: The flag of each nation has colors with special meanings. Study them to find out what they are.

What other colors that you see every day have a particular meaning? Will those colors have the same meaning to someone in another country?

Here are some of the ways that different cultures interpret colors. What's happy for one could be sad for another. Be careful what colors you wear!

WHITE
Asia—death, bad luck

India—sorrow

Navajo—dawn, east

Peru—health

Western cultures—elegance, weddings

Worldwide—peace

RED
Asia—marriage, prosperity, happiness

India—purity, marriage

Ivory Coast Africa—death

Muslim culture—heat

New Zealand—nobility, divinity

South Africa—mourning

Western cultures—love, passion, anger

BLACK
African cultures—maturity

Asia—knowledge

China—little boys

European cultures—rebellion

Navajo—night, north

Thailand—bad luck

Western cultures—mourning, respect

ORANGE
Asia—courage, health

Egypt—mourning

India—fire, luck

Western cultures—fun, creativity

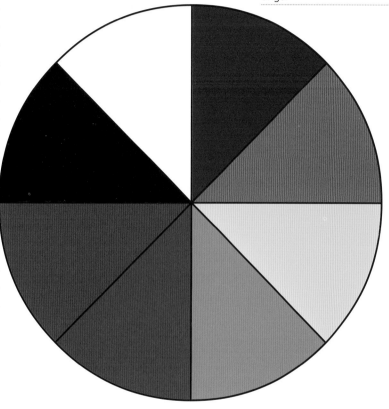

PURPLE
Iran—the future

Japan—enlightenment

Latin America—death

Thailand—mourning

Ukraine—faith

United States—honor and courage

Western cultures—royalty and wealth

YELLOW
China—honor, royalty

Egypt—happiness and good fortune

Europe—cowardice, jealousy

Hindu cultures—spring

Japan—courage

Navajo—dusk, west

Western cultures—cheerfulness

BLUE
China—girls

Egypt—divinity

France—royalty

Iran—mourning

Middle East—safety, healing

Navajo—daytime, south

Western cultures—boys, trust, sadness

GREEN
China—virtue

Ireland—patriotism

Islamic cultures—luck

Japan—new life

Western cultures—spring, jealousy, luck

Worldwide—ecology

NAME THAT COLOR

One of the fun challenges for companies producing new products—everything from cars to nail polish—is to come up with new names for colors, such as Sizzling Red, Poison Green, or Burrito Brown. Here's an experiment: Give each of the colors here a name based on what you think of when you see the color. First impressions are best! Write down the names. How do you think each color should be used? Write that down too. Then, show the colors to your friends and ask them to do the same. Did they have the same associations with the colors that you did?

CHAPTER 2

SHADOW AND LIGHT

Leonardo drew many studies of light reflections on curved mirrors in his notebooks. On the right-hand page, Leonardo details that in using concave mirrors of equal diameter, "the one that has a shallower curve will concentrate the highest number of reflected rays on to a focal point, and as a consequence, it will kindle a fire with greater rapidity and force."

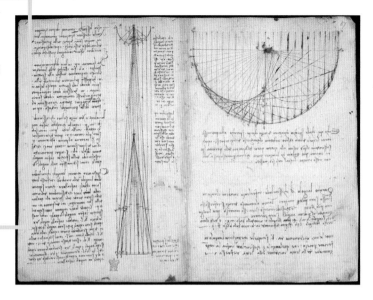

THE NATURE OF LIGHT

Every artist has to consider light in creating paintings and sculpture, but Leonardo was interested in light from a scientific point of view as well. He realized that if he understood how shadows and reflections worked scientifically, he could make realistic use of them in his paintings.

Leonardo filled page after page of his notebooks with studies of the way light travels and reflects back at us. He knew that light travels from its source in straight lines and reflects back toward us at specific angles when it hits a surface. And because he was always looking for connections, Leonardo also discovered in his studies that the same laws that govern the reflection of light also govern the bouncing of a ball and the rebounding of sound when it hits a surface.

BENDING LIGHT

As a boy in Andrea del Verrocchio's studio, Leonardo knew how to make good use of light's straight lines of travel. He learned to grind glass lenses and use curved mirrors to focus sunlight (and its heat) onto a surface. In doing so, he could use the light beam to start fires or to heat and melt solder for welding metal sculpture.

Convex lenses and mirrors curve outward. Concave lenses and mirrors curve inward. The two types of shaped surfaces focus and reflect light differently. The convex lens (on the left) bends the light inward so that it concentrates into a single point and then reverses; the concave lens (on the right) bends the light outward so that it spreads.

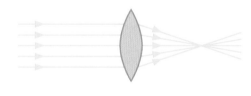

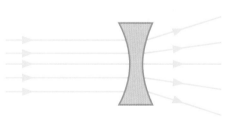

Leonardo used these principles not only to focus light (with convex lenses) to heat surfaces but also to reflect light (with concave lenses) for reading. He designed lamps that greatly increased the spread of light from a lamp or candle flame by placing a curved mirror behind it.

USING REFLECTION TO CHANGE LIGHT

Here are two ways to experiment with the direction and effects of light.

EXPERIMENT 1: MAGNIFY LIGHT WITH A FLEXIBLE PLASTIC MIRROR

Find out what happens when you use curved mirror surfaces to reflect light. For this first experiment you'll need a sheet of flexible plastic mirror—available at art and craft supply stores, hardware stores, and online.

WHAT YOU WILL NEED

Human power: Do this with two friends.

1 sheet 8½" × 11" (21.5 × 28 cm) white cardstock

1 sheet 6" × 9" (15 × 23 cm) flexible plastic mirror

2 rubber bands

Flashlight

Notebook and pencil

Note: You will need to do this experiment in a darkened room.

1 Ask Friend 1 to hold up the piece of white cardstock while Friend 2 holds the sheet of plastic mirror, facing the cardstock. Make sure they're both held flat, at the same level.

2 Shine a flashlight at the mirror. Notice the light that reflects onto the white cardstock. Write down what you see.

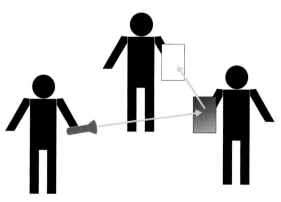

3 Ask Friend 2 to bend the mirror so that it curves away from the cardstock (convex). Use a rubber band or two to hold it in the curved position. How did it change? Write down what you notice.

4 Now ask Friend 2 to bend the mirror so that it curves toward the cardstock (concave). How did it change? Write down what you observe.

WHAT IS HAPPENING?

When the mirror is flat, the light reflects evenly to the white surface. When the mirror is convex, the light diffuses in different directions. But, when the mirror is concave, the light becomes focused on the white surface.

EXPERIMENT 2: SPREAD LIGHT WITH WHITE PAPER

Reflected light illuminates differently from direct light. Try this experiment with two friends, indoors, in a room that can be darkened slightly.

WHAT YOU WILL NEED

Chair

Flashlight (or small table lamp without a lampshade)

Large white poster board

1 Have your friend sit in a chair.

2 Darken the room slightly. Turn on the flashlight and shine it toward your friend's face. (Not directly in the eyes!) Notice how the direct light makes harsh shadows.

3 Have a second friend hold up a sheet of white poster board near your first friend's face. Aim the light at the poster board so that the light reflects onto your friend's face but does not fall on it directly. What happens to the shadows on the face? Move the poster board at different angles until you find the spot that creates the brightest glow on their face. What are the shadows like?

WHAT IS HAPPENING?

You changed the effect of lighting and shadows with reflected light. Portrait photographers often use this technique for softer lighting to make a model's face appear younger.

LIGHT AND THE EYE

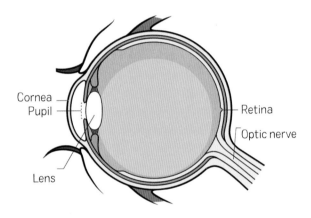

Cornea

Pupil

Lens

Retina

Optic nerve

LET'S SEE

We need light not only to perceive color but also to see everything else around us. An interesting phenomenon happens in the process of seeing, because if it were only up to our eyes, we'd see everything upside down! We need our brains to turn everything right-side up again.

HOW DOES THAT WORK?

Light enters the eye through the *cornea*, the clear protective covering on the front of eye. The cornea directs light through the *pupil*. The pupil looks like a black dot in the center of the *iris*—the colorful part of the eye. But it's not a dot; it's an opening that can become smaller or larger to let in less light or more.

The pupil directs the light to the *lens* immediately behind it. The lens, in turn, directs the light to the *retina* at the back of the eye. The retina has receptor cells called rods and cones that "read," or picture, what we are looking at—upside down.

WHY UPSIDE DOWN?

If you had an eyecube instead of an eyeball, the surfaces of the eye and lens would be flat. Light would pass through the lens just like it passes through a window in your house, and the image that it sends to the retina would be right-side up.

But the eye and the lens are convex, and when light passes through them, it refracts—bends—so that the angles cross and the image reverses. The cells in the retina then send electrical impulses to the brain through the *optic nerve*, which turns the image upright again.

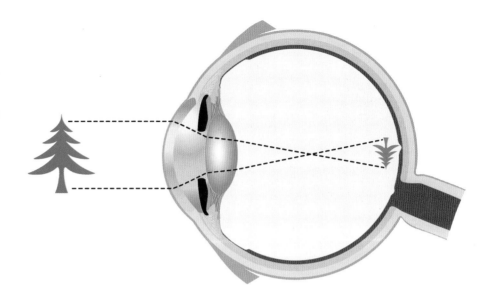

THE EYE OF THE CAMERA

From the very beginning, in the 19th Century, cameras were designed to function just like the eye within a box. A lens cap protected the lens like the cornea does the eye. The camera's aperture, or opening, functions like the eye's pupil—both the aperture and the pupil can adapt to changing light conditions. The camera's lens focuses light onto the back surface inside the camera, just as the eye's lens does on the retina. Cameras originally had a glass plate or film lining the back, which recorded the image.

Just as it happens in the eye, the image turned upside down once it passed through the camera's lens, but a camera didn't require a brain to turn the image right-side up. When you removed the glass plate or film and processed it to print the photograph, you simply turned the photograph right-side up yourself.

BUILD A CAMERA OBSCURA

WHAT YOU WILL NEED

Cardboard box (a shoebox will work fine)

2" (5 cm)-wide roll duct tape

Pencil

Ruler

Utility knife (ask an adult for help)

Self-healing cutting mat

Scissors

Wax paper

Heavy aluminum foil

Pin

Tack

Large piece of opaque cloth (a towel or tablecloth will work)

Test the process for yourself by building a camera obscura, which means "dark chamber." Artists and scientists have been intrigued with the camera obscura since even before Leonardo's time, sometimes creating an enormous one by using an actual chamber, or room, in a house as the box.

The simplest camera obscuras work with the use of a pinhole as the aperture to let the light into the box. The tiny hole, literally made with the point of a pin, is so small that it condenses the light rays and reverses the image. You can also experiment with this project using an inexpensive magnifying lens behind the aperture.

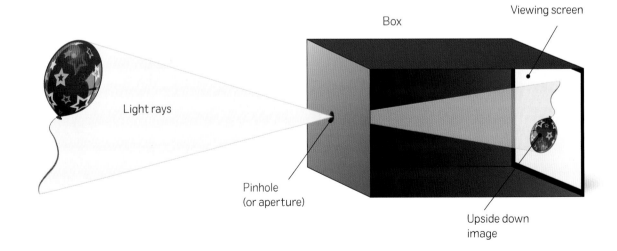

Box

Viewing screen

Light rays

Pinhole (or aperture)

Upside down image

PREPARE THE BOX:

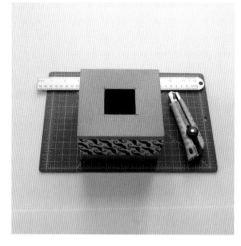

1   Use duct tape to seal the box. Cover all openings, including edges, seams, and corners.

2   Draw a 2" × 2" (5 × 5 cm) square in the center of each end of the box.

3   With the utility knife, cut out the two squares. One will be the viewing window, and the other will be the aperture.

MAKE THE VIEWING WINDOW:

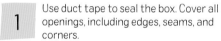

1   Use scissors to cut a 3" × 3" (7.5 × 7.5 cm) square of wax paper.

2   Place the piece of wax paper over one of the 2" (5 cm) holes, taping it to the box with duct tape.

MAKE THREE APERTURES:

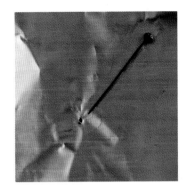
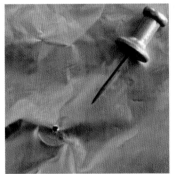
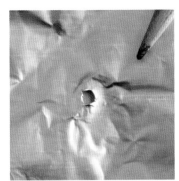

1 Use scissors to cut three 3" × 3" (7.5 × 7.5 cm) squares of aluminum foil.

2 Make one aperture in the center of each of the squares.

A. Use a pin to poke a tiny hole—an aperture of about $\frac{1}{32}$" (0.8 mm) diameter.

B. Use a tack to poke a small hole—an aperture of about $\frac{1}{16}$" (0.16 mm) diameter.

C. Use a pencil point to poke a slightly larger hole—an aperture of about $\frac{1}{8}$" (3 mm) diameter.

3 Place the square of foil with the smallest aperture over the second hole in the box. Make sure the aperture is centered over the hole.

4 Use duct tape to attach it to the box. Seal all of the edges so light will only enter through the hole. Set aside the other two apertures for later.

GET READY TO VIEW:

1 Turn on a lamp. Hold the camera with the aperture facing the lamp. The wax-paper viewing window should be about 8" (20 cm) away from your eyes.

2 Use the fabric to cover your head and the viewing end of the box to block the light from your eyes. Don't cover the aperture with the cloth.

3 Look steadily at the viewing window. Shortly, you will see an image of the lamp. What do you notice? Is the image right-side up or upside down? Is the image reversed? What is the light level? Is the image clear and crisp?

4 Change the aperture and try the experiment again.

5 Record your observations. The smaller the aperture, the smaller and sharper the image will be. A larger aperture increases the image size, but the image is less focused. Why? When the aperture is larger, the rays crowd inside from different angles, making the image faint and fuzzy but magnified.

MAKE IT BIGGER!
Find out what happens to the image when you place an inexpensive magnifying glass behind the aperture. Use tape to attach the glass next to the aperture inside of the box.

BIGGER YET!
Create a huge camera obscura, one you and a friend can sit in, using an extra-large box.

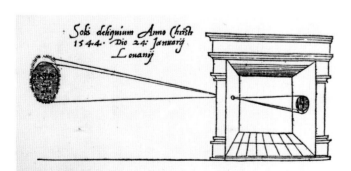

This drawing, from January 1544, is the first published illustration of a camera obscura, and a room-size one at that. The illustration shows that the camera was used to observe a solar eclipse.

THE NATURE OF SHADOWS

Detail of the hands in the *Mona Lisa*, circa 1503–06.

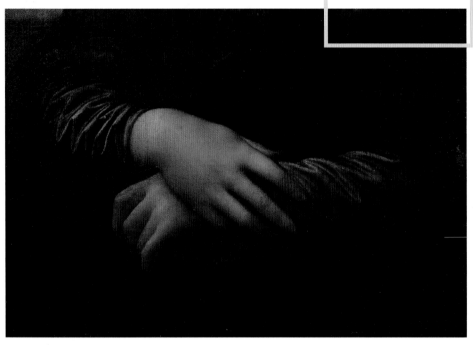

DEFINING A SHADOW

A shadow is created when something partially or completely gets in the way of a light source. You can explore shadow making in its simplest form by making shadow portraits, or silhouettes, with your friends.

"Shadow is the means by which bodies display their form," Leonardo wrote, meaning that it's the shadows that allow us to perceive something's three-dimensional qualities. Most of us don't give a whole lot of thought to shadows, but Leonardo did. He wrote pages and pages about them in his notebooks.

He realized that understanding shadow is extremely important to an artist. Light allows us to see color, but without shadow, we would only see one flat tone of each color.

Without shadows, the *Mona Lisa*'s hands, shown here, would look flat and uniformly beige, as if they were cut out of a piece of construction paper and stuck into place. It's the shadows that create variations in tone. They allow the hands to look three dimensional and the fingers rounded, as if you could reach into the painting and shake her hand.

Look closely at the *Mona Lisa*'s fingers, and you'll see something else Leonardo did—the shadows are not all the same color. "Shadow may be infinitely dark, and also of infinite degrees of absence of darkness," he wrote. They vary from light to near-black shades of the base color. The beige of hands grows gradually darker the farther you get from the light source.

DRAW A SILHOUETTE

All you need is a large sheet of paper, masking tape, a table lamp, a stool or low-backed chair, a friend, and a pencil. Tape the paper to a wall. Place the lamp on a table several feet away and set the stool in between the lamp and the wall. Ask your friend to sit down, and turn on the lamp so that your friend's shadow is cast onto the drawing paper. You might have to adjust the height of the paper or the distance of the lamp from the wall several times before you're happy with the shadow. You can also use the angle of the light to create an interesting elongated shadow.

Use the pencil to trace the outline of the shadow (don't fuss too much with the details or your friend will get tired of posing). When you remove the paper from the wall, enjoy the drawing as is or cut it out along the outline and glue it to a contrasting colored background. Black on white and white on black are traditional for silhouette portraits.

You can also try this outdoors, using your camera to help you experiment with shadows. Try photographing the same pose at different times of day.

This special chair and screen combination was advertised as a "Sure and Convenient Machine for Drawing Silhouettes," circa 1790.

SHADOW CRAZE

Beginning in the late 1700s, there was an absolute craze for shadow portraits—it lasted for decades! Artists traveled with their "silhouette machines," which they could set up in people's homes. An entire family might have portraits done, most often as miniatures. The artist could control the size of the portrait by adjusting the distance of the light and the sitter from the transparent screen. Drawing paper was attached on the opposite side of the screen, where the artist traced the outline. The portrait was then inked in or cut out and attached to another piece of paper.

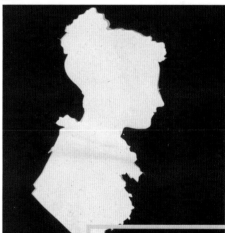

Silhouette of Sarah Faraday (1800–79) from the scrapbook of her husband, scientist Michael Faraday, 1821.

MAKE SHADOW PUPPETS

WHAT YOU WILL NEED

Pencil

Paper

Sheets of heavy cardstock or cardboard

Scissors or utility knife (ask an adult for help)

Thin wooden dowels

Duct tape

Hole punch

Brass fasteners

String

White sheet

Lamp with a bare bulb

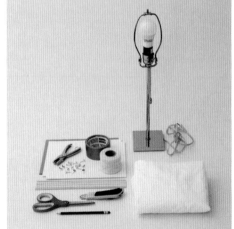

Puppets allow you to explore what shadows can do through storytelling—an art that originated in China over 1,000 years ago.

Stage a shadow-puppet show with your friends by dramatizing a favorite tale—or write an original play with your own cast of shadowy characters.

For this activity you'll need to hang a white sheet from a doorway or clothesline. Your audience will sit on one side of the sheet, and you and your fellow actors will be on the other side of the sheet with a light source behind you. You'll lie on your back and manipulate the puppets with sticks. (The Muppets are controlled this way too.)

Consider making your puppets at least 10" or 12" (25 or 30.5 cm) in size so that they can be easily and clearly seen by the audience on the other side of the sheet. By exaggerating things like big hair, big noses, and long, skinny legs, you'll also help the audience understand the characters.

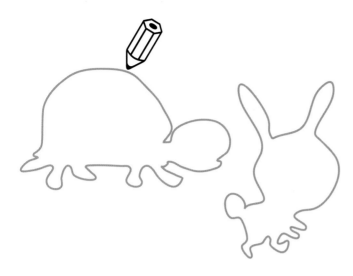

1 Make a list of the characters that will appear in your play. Decide which characters need to have moving parts and which do not.

2 For characters that don't need any moving parts, simply draw the outline of the character on a piece of cardstock or cardboard, paying special attention to hairdos, hats, arm and leg positions, tails, and other details that help to define the character. Cut along the outline with scissors or a utility knife. Lay the puppet flat, wrong-side up, center a piece of dowel on the puppet, and attach it with duct tape.

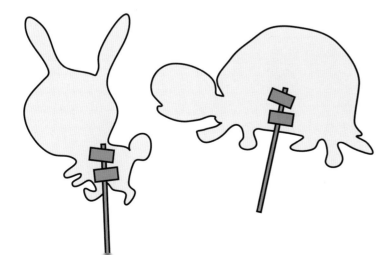

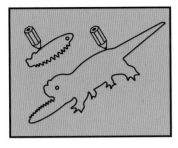 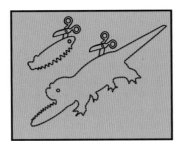

3 For characters that need to have legs, arms, jaws, or wings that move, draw the main body of the character on cardboard. Then, draw the parts that need to move separately. For instance, if you need arms that move, draw one part as shoulder to elbow, then another part as elbow to fingers. Be sure to leave about ½" (1.3 cm) extra space where the pieces need to overlap at the joints.

4 Cut out the individual parts and use the hole punch to make a clean hole at each place where the pieces need to overlap. Join the pieces by inserting and opening a brass fastener.

5 Lay the puppet wrong-side up. Use duct tape to attach one dowel to the body of the character and one dowel to each limb. For a puppet with two arms that move, for instance, you'll need one dowel for the body and one for each arm.

6 Now, get behind the sheet, turn on the light, lie on your back, and hold up your puppets. Have someone turn off the other lights in the room and check on the other side of the sheet to make sure the puppets' shadows are clear.

7 Let the show begin.

TAKE IT FURTHER

Try some experiments to make your shadow-puppet theater work to the max.

1 Move the puppets close to the screen. What happens to the shadow? Move the puppets away from the screen. How does the shadow change?

2 Move the light. Play with the angle and position of the light. Have a friend move the light while you watch the shadows. What happens to the shadows when the light is moving?

3 Add some color to the shadows using plastic color sheets. Cut out some color silhouettes. Place them in the puppet theater with the other puppets. Or, add a touch of color to the puppets, by taping the plastic to parts to them.

POSER:
It takes about 24 frames to make on second of film. How many pictures would you need to make the sixty-five-minute movie?

4 Project the shadows onto a wall. How can you make a dark shadow? A faint shadow?

5 Make a backdrop scene inside the puppet theater. Animate the puppets in front of the scene.

This is a still from *The Adventures of Prince Achmet* by Lotte Reiniger, 1919. Notice how carefully the shapes have been cut.

SILHOUETTE ANIMATION

In 1926, German artist and director Charlotte "Lotte" Reiniger created one of the first animated shadow-puppet movies, titled *The Adventures of Prince Achmet*. In making the film, she invented a technique called silhouette animation, a form of stop-motion animation. She cut out intricate silhouettes and brought the fairy tale to life by compiling thousands of photos into a silent film.

CHIAROSCURO DRAWING

WHAT KIND OF DRAWING?

It's pronounced kyarro-skooro, and in Italian, it means "light-dark." For artists, chiaroscuro is the contrast of light and shadow that makes a painting or drawing appear three dimensional. In Leonardo's opinion, creating an image that appears to come away from the surface realistically was the primary goal of a painter.

At first, as a young apprentice learning his skills in Verrocchio's studio, Leonardo didn't get to work on the faces and hands in important paintings. He had the task of painting people's clothing, while the master artist painted the people themselves. Yet in painting fabrics and clothing, Leonardo realized that capturing accurate shadows was the most important thing in making a painting so realistic you can almost feel it.

Leonardo's study of draped fabric makes beautiful use of chiaroscuro, circa 1475–80

Portrait of Simonetta Vespucci as a Nymph
by Sandro Botticelli, 1485.

Portrait of a Lady from the Court of Milan
by Leonardo da Vinci, circa 1490–95.

IT'S ALL BLACK AND WHITE

Chiaroscuro is used for modeling in paintings with plenty of color, but it's easiest to grasp its effects when you try it in black and white. Try it yourself with pictures of silver that you find in magazines. You'll need some black or gray drawing paper, and some black and white chalk or pastels.

Start with a faint outline sketch of the object. Then begin to draw in the gradations of tone in the photo, starting with the brightest whites and gradually moving through all the shades of gray to the deepest blacks. It can be useful to use cotton swabs, or to a wrap a soft cloth or tissue over your index finger to blend the tones of the pastels. Who knew black + white = silver?

This was the opposite of the way most artists thought and worked in his day. They relied on outlines to create the three-dimensional look. You can see the difference in these two paintings. The one on the left is a portrait of Simonetta Vespucci (Amerigo's sister) painted by Sandro Botticelli in 1485. The one on the right, by Leonardo in 1490, is thought to be a portrait of Lucrezia Crivelli from Milan.

Both portraits are beautiful, but notice how Botticelli created each shape with outline and then filled in the color. Leonardo's portrait is full of soft edges. He used his chiaroscuro shading to make the young woman's nose, chin, and the folds in her velvet sleeves appear naturally rounded.

DRAW AN ALL-WHITE STILL LIFE

Explore the effects of shadow and lighting by setting up and drawing a still life with no color at all.

WHAT YOU WILL NEED

Large sheets of white paper or a white tablecloth

White objects for a still life (such as dishes, mugs, boxes, clothing, or 3D shapes you make from paper)

Flashlight

Sketchpad

Pencil

1 Cover a tabletop with the white paper or tablecloth. Arrange a still-life scene on top with whatever objects you have. Maybe it's a couple of empty white gift boxes, a ball, and a cylinder or cone you form out of a piece of white paper.

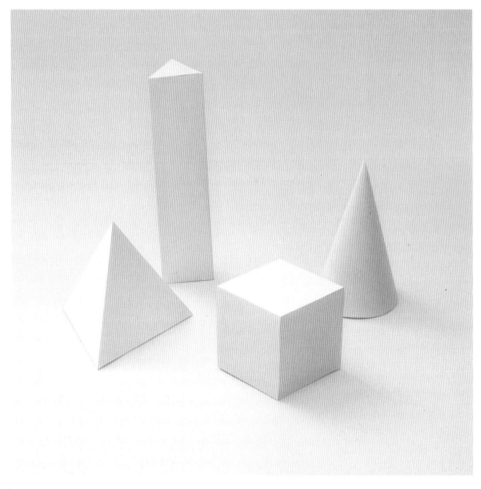

2 Darken the room. Aim a flashlight or a lamp at the still life.

3 Draw what you see, using shading to create the objects' dimension.

TRY THIS:

Adjust the light source in different ways. What do you notice about the shading and shadow when the light is close to the objects? What happens when the light is far away from the objects? What happens when the light source is behind the objects? How can you make the shadows longer or shorter?

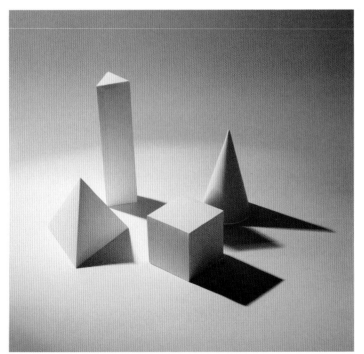

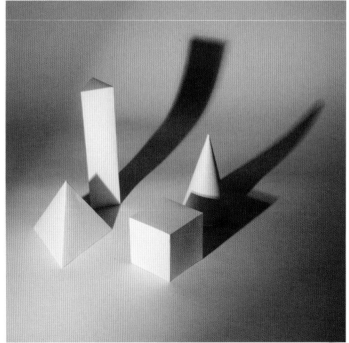

FIVE O'CLOCK SHADOW

Clocks were not easy to carry around in Leonardo's day. This is his design for a mechanical clock.

HARNESSING SHADOWS

Mechanical clocks existed in Leonardo's day, but they were very large, very heavy, and very rare. People didn't have clocks in their homes or most places where they worked, but they were still able to tell time. The position of the sun and shadows were all they needed.

In the morning, when the sun appears low in the eastern sky, shadows are long and fall to the west.

As the afternoon progresses, the Earth turns, the sun appears slightly farther west in the sky, and the angle of the sun's rays changes. Shadows grow gradually longer.

At noon, when the sun is directly overhead, shadows fall straight down. The shadows under these beach umbrellas suggest that it's just about noon.

By midafternoon, the shadow is complete, showing the whole form of the object it belongs to.

And finally, in the late afternoon, as the sun nears time for setting in the west, the shadows become wonderfully exaggerated as they fall to the east.

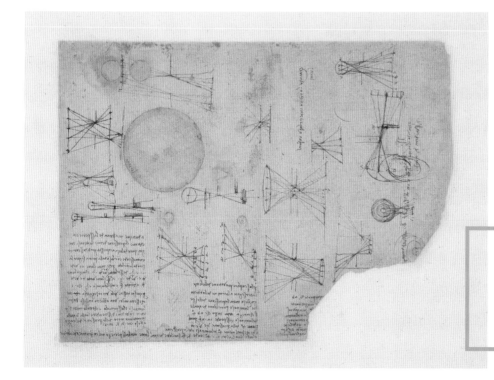

If you lived at a time when no one had a watch or a clock and certainly not a cellphone, you would learn to tell the time very quickly with a glance at your shadow or someone else's.

In fact, your shadow performs more like a clock than you might realize. As shadows change throughout the day, moving from west in the morning to east in the afternoon, they move in a clockwise rotation.

Leonardo was fascinated with light and shadow. His sketches here show how shadows change with different angles of light.

MAKE YOUR OWN SUNDIAL

Before mechanical clocks, people used a stick inserted into the ground and the shadows it cast to tell time. This works, as you just read, because shadows move in a clockwise direction throughout the day.

People discovered that a shadow stick, or *gnomon**, were most accurate when the stick was inserted in the ground at an angle. It turned out there was a reason for that: The Earth's axis is also at an angle. The angle of the stick needs to correspond to the angle of the Earth's latitude in the part of the world where you live. So, to make your sundial, you first need to find out your latitude.

Gnomon, from the ancient Greek, means "one who knows."

For a sundial to be accurate, the angle of the shadow stick, or gnomon, needs to match the angle of the latitude where the sundial is located.

RIDDLE:
The sundial is the timepiece with the fewest parts. What is the timepiece with the most parts?

ANSWER:
An hourglass. Each piece of sand is a part!

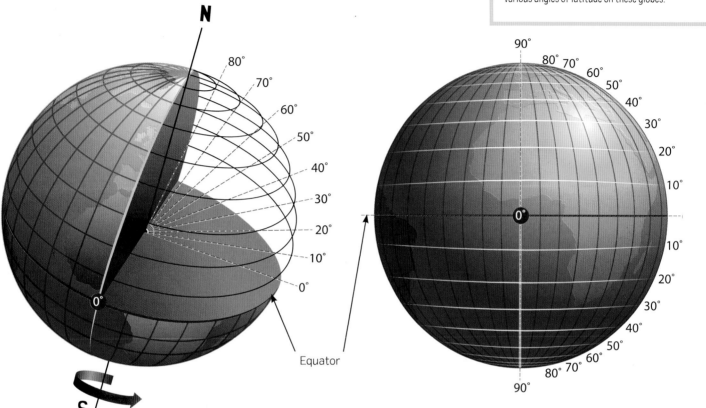

Equator

FIND YOUR LATITUDE:

You'll want to start by looking up your latitude in an atlas or online. Marrakech, for instance is 31.6 degrees, London is 51.50, Melbourne is 37.8, Paris is 48.8, Montevideo is 34.9, and Tokyo is 35.68. Write down the figure for the area where you live and save it.

FIND YOUR SURFACE AND STICK:

Next, do a little outdoor investigation. Find a flat piece of ground where you can keep your sundial setup. Bare ground is best, so that you can see the markers that you'll be using. You'll also need to find a sturdy stick—maybe a foot in length or longer. It could be part of an old broom handle, or a garden stake, or a straight stick from a tree.

If it's sturdy enough, you might be able to have someone help you sharpen one end of it with a utility knife and pound it into the ground with a hammer. If not, you'll need a trowel or shovel to dig a hole for it, and then pack the pack the dirt back in around it tightly. But not yet! Right now, just find the piece of ground and the stick.

TIME:

Start this project on a sunny morning. Setup takes 20 minuteEllen Callaway / Callaway Photoery hour you record will take 5 minutes or less.

WHAT YOU WILL NEED

Black marker

One sheet of paper

Pebbles
(about 50 to 60)

Protractor

Stick

Navigational
compass

Clock or watch
with an alarm

1 Bring the materials on the list to your flat area of ground.

2 Select twelve pebbles. Use the marker to label each pebble with a number, 1 through 12. These will mark the time on the sundial.

3 Use the compass to find north, and lay the stick on the ground so it is pointing that direction.

4 Find your angle of latitude on the protractor. Angle the stick into the ground at the same angle as the latitude. Make sure the stick is still pointing north. You just lined up the gnomon with the Earth's axis.

5 Set the alarm on the clock or watch to go off every hour, on the hour.

WHAT'S GOING ON?

The Earth constantly rotates slowly on its axis in an eastward direction. Sundials measure the Earth's rotation every day. Shadows change because the Earth is rotating as it orbits the sun. The shadow's length and the number of sunlight hours will always be changing—hour to hour, day to day, and place to place—as the Earth rotates.

6 When the alarm goes off, look at the stick's shadow. Wherever the shadow is, beginning at the base of the stick, place a line of pebbles that records the length of the shadow. At the end of each shadow, place the numbered pebble that represents the time. On paper, record the time of day and the position of the sun.

7 Repeat this every hour throughout the day.

Look at the pattern you made with the pebbles. Where was the sun in the sky when the shadow was the shortest? Longest? Are the numbers on your sundial in clockwise order?

CHAPTER 3

LINES
AND PATTERNS

FOLLOWING THE LINE

The Swiss artist Paul Klee (1879–1940) once said, "A line is a dot that went for a walk." And he was right. Line up an infinite series of tiny points, or dots, to form a line, and they can go in any direction imaginable. A line invites you to follow it.

A single line can suggest a vast landscape.

Mural from the *Temple of Longing Thither* by Paul Klee, 1922, painted in watercolor and ink.

THE LANGUAGE OF LINES

Lines are used descriptively in language, but the drawn line also has its own visual language—like a code. You can use lines to communicate ideas, motion, symbolic meanings, and senses. They can be drawn to describe something real or abstract. They can also describe surfaces, textures, patterns, or values of light and shadow. Lines are important visual elements in describing the things we see.

FIFTEEN WAYS TO USE LINE

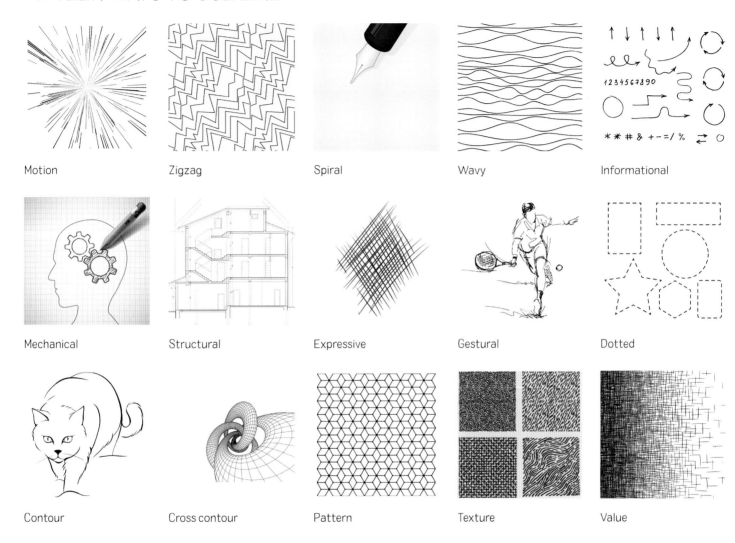

Motion

Zigzag

Spiral

Wavy

Informational

Mechanical

Structural

Expressive

Gestural

Dotted

Contour

Cross contour

Pattern

Texture

Value

LOOK FOR YOURSELF. TRY THESE QUICK LINE-MIND EXPERIMENTS:

Draw a horizontal line. What does it communicate to you? Does it suggest the horizon? A slit cut into a piece of paper? Maybe it makes you think of a piece of a short path or a piece of spaghetti.

Rotate the line so it is standing up straight or leaning at a diagonal. What does it say now? Do you see a hill? Maybe you imagine something growing up, falling down, or launching into space?

Next, draw 95 percent of a circle. Look at the missing part—this is what's called an implied line. An implied line is a line that's not visibly there. When two ends of a line are close to meeting, the brain does a special trick to visually connect them. When a line connects, it makes a shape.

MEANINGFUL LINES

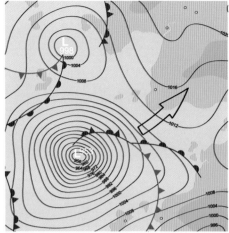

You've seen many of the lines from the chart before. Think of all the traffic maps and weather maps you've seen on the news. All of those straight, swirling, concentric, dotted, and directional lines mean something. Can you figure out what the lines are telling you without any voice over or printed explanations?

HOW WOULD YOU EXPLAIN THE WEATHER WITH LINES?

Invent your own meaningful lines for forecasting the weather. How would you indicate a cold front on its way? How about a heat wave, thunderstorm, overcast skies, or fluctuating temperatures? Jot them down on a piece of paper.

TRY IT ON YOUR FRIENDS

Draw a simple outline map of your region, or the whole country. Then, with colored markers, and using your newly invented weather lines, draw the approaching weather on your map. Now, present the map to your friends. See if they can tell what kind of weather is on the way based on your meaningful lines.

Lines are so familiar that we use them in many different ways in language as well as in art. What kinds of lines do these descriptions bring to mind?

1. What kind of line is annoying?
2. What do you refuse to cross?
3. What do you like to cross?
4. What waits for your signature?
5. What suggests the best of the best?
6. What's another word for a slogan?
7. What do you do when you behave?
8. What do you do when you misbehave?
9. What do you do when you figure something out?
10. What do you do when you change the rules?

REINVENTING THE LINE—MAKE YOUR OWN DRAWING TOOLS

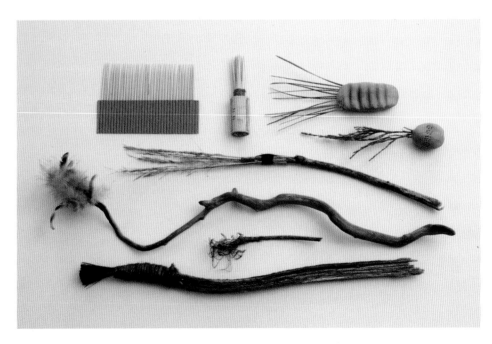

In this project you'll explore the infinite variety in the weight, color, shape, and feeling of line by creating your own brushes and mark makers from things around the house and yard. You can do this by yourself, but it's even more fun with a friend.

We'll do this in two parts, first to make the drawing tools, then to see what happens when you draw the lines.

GET GATHERING

Get inventive and start gathering materials that you can use to make brushes and other drawing and painting tools. You'll be able to keep these tools for a long time, so you don't have to make them all at once. Keep adding to your very special (and slightly weird) supply of art tools. Here are some ideas, but don't be limited by them. Think of other materials that you could use, too.

MATERIALS FOR TOOL HANDLES

Tree branches

Bamboo garden stakes

Chopsticks

Knitting needles

Stiff cardboard

Stone

Plastic forks and spoons

Pencils

Heavy wire

Kitchen utensils

MATERIALS FOR TOOL TIPS

Feathers

Toothpicks

Rags

Pine needles

Dried weeds/grasses

Cotton ball/swabs

Tangled string

Sponges

Plastic scrubbers

Lint

MATERIALS FOR ATTACHING TIPS TO HANDLES

String

Yarn

Embroidery thread

Leather strips

Wire

Twine

Air-dry clay

Wax

Hot/craft glue

Various kinds of tape cut into strips

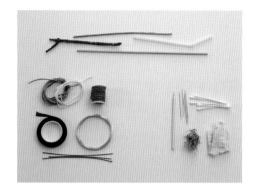

Lay out all of your materials, according to use. Pick a handle, pick a tip material, and think about the best way to join them. You might want to create some tools that are like brushes. You could hot-glue feathers or grass onto the end of a stick and then wrap the glued end with string to keep all the feathers in place, then tie off the ends of the string.

You might want to create other tools that are more like combs. For that type, you could cut a piece of corrugated cardboard to fit comfortably in your hand. Dip the ends of toothpicks into craft glue, insert them partway into the corrugated openings along one side, and allow the glue to dry. Hold the cardboard like a comb when you dip the toothpicks into ink to make multiple lines.

For a 3D tool, you could put a wad of air-dry clay at the end of a stick and use it to insert twigs at every angle. Allow the clay to air dry.

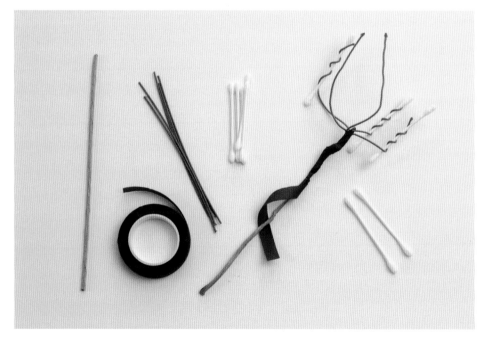

GET CREATIVE! YOUR TOOLS ARE YOURS ALONE—THEY WON'T LOOK LIKE ANYONE ELSE'S.

NOW LET'S MAKE SOME LINES

The process could get messy, so protect your work surface by covering it with paper or plastic and put on an old T-shirt or apron.

WHAT YOU WILL NEED

India ink or sumi ink

Water

Large sheets of newspaper, drawing paper, or watercolor paper

2 bowls

1 Pour a small amount of ink into one bowl and water into another.

2 Test the drawing tool. Dip the drawing tool tip into the water first, so the tip is moist; this will help to pull ink into the tip. Then, dip the tip into the ink and try drawing.

3 Make different values of gray ink by diluting the ink with different amounts of water in different bowls, from pale gray to deep black.

4 Try out the process with the other tools. Think about which kind of line would be the most expressive for different kinds of images.

MAKE YOUR OWN INK!

India ink is made of carbon particles suspended in water. It's permanent and archival, meaning it will last a very, very long time. You can make it yourself.

Collect some burnt charcoal from hardwood (a small handful will be enough) and pulverize the charcoal into a fine dust using a mortar and pestle. Add five to ten drops of water to the charcoal dust and mix with a spoon or stick. Continue to add drops of water, then mix, until it is the consistency of light cream. You're ready to draw.

LINES THAT DEFINE

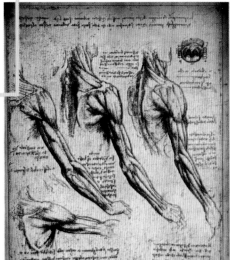

Leonardo had strong opinions about using shadow, rather than line, to create a believable three-dimensional quality in a painting—but that doesn't mean that he didn't use line in his art. In fact, Leonardo used line all the time in his nature drawings, in his anatomical studies of humans and animals, in his technical plans for engineering projects, and in sketches for painting. He was a master of line.

Mastering line means that with something as simple as a pencil, you can create lines that are light, dark, delicate, bold, straight edged, flowing, silky, or sharp. You can draw lines that seem to be coming toward you, and lines that appear to fade away in the distance. You can convey the idea that something is soft or hard to the touch.

Artists use line as a way to define on paper what they see in front of them or in their imaginations. A line can define the shapes, volumes, surfaces, and textures of the things we see. In order to help train their eyes and hands to work together when drawing, artists practice by doing different types of drawing exercises.

One of the exercises, which is all about using line, is called contour drawing—and you can do it, too.

CONTOUR DRAWING

A contour drawing helps you get a feel for the overall shapes of a subject by paying close attention to the edges, wrinkles, and crevices and drawing them without any shadows.

You might start a contour drawing by picking up your pencil or marker and focusing on something in nature, or a corner of your room, or the things on the breakfast table. You're going to draw what you see with just with outlines. Look back and forth from the subject to your paper as you go along.

Even though the drawing is simple, without shading or too much detail, try to capture the feeling of what you're looking at with your lines. For instance, in this drawing of wildflowers in a meadow, you get a sense of the delicacy of the petals and stems by the way their outlines waver naturally. You can sense the flowers at the top of the drawing reaching for the sun and feel the depth of the meadow by the way the stems overlap each other and some of the flowers. The drawing captures a lot with just simple line.

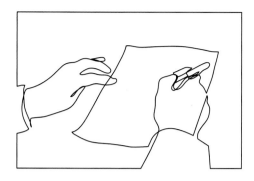

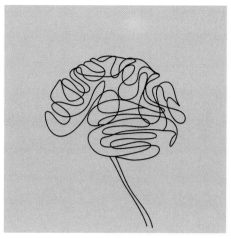

CONTINUOUS-LINE CONTOUR DRAWING

Now make the exercise a little more challenging, and a little more fun. A continuous line drawing is made—you guessed it—with one continuous line. Once your pencil or marker touches the paper, it stays in contact with the paper until the drawing is done. Draw as you did in the first exercise, following the contours of the subject you're looking at. Sometimes the lines will overlap as if you're seeing through the drawing to the other side.

To draw subjects that don't stand still, like the bicyclist, work with photos in magazines or online.

Once you get the hang of continuous-line drawing, give yourself a time limit. Try doing a complete drawing in one minute—then try it in thirty seconds. You'll see rapid improvement in your mastery of line.

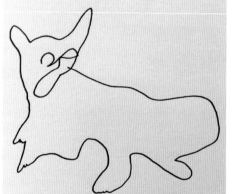

BLIND CONTOUR DRAWING

Ready for the next level of challenge? Try a blind contour drawing.

For this type of drawing, you don't get to look at your paper. Keep your eyes on the subject the whole time. It's definitely best if you do it as a continuous line drawing without picking up your pencil.

Resist the urge to sneak a peek at the drawing before it is finished. The reward will be a wonderful surprise because the drawing will look like an abstract version of the subject.

For extra fun, get your friends together and make blind contour portraits of each other.

LINES IN SPACE

Have you ever thought of drawing or writing with lines in the air without a pencil or pen? With just your hands, some wire, and a pair of pliers, you can explore contour drawing in space.

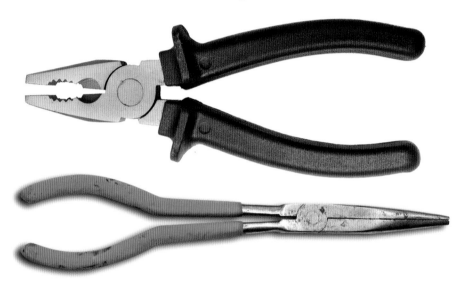

CHOOSING WIRE:

Craft wire comes in many thicknesses—called gauges—and different degrees of hardness. Steel wire is much harder to bend than aluminum wire. Some wire, like fine copper wire, is very easy to bend but it doesn't hold its shape very well. Other wire, like the steel wire that coat hangers are made of, is too hard to bend successfully into the shapes you want.

For this project, a 16-gauge aluminum (natural or black finish) or copper wire should be just right. You can find it at craft or hardware stores. A 20-gauge steel wire is also workable and will hold its shape, but it is much thinner than the 16-gauge and will not create a substantial-looking line. Test a small piece of wire before you buy it to see if it's the right weight for you. Feel free to use any other kind of wire that works for you.

CHOOSING PLIERS:

Ordinary pliers will bend and cut 16-gauge aluminum wire very easily. A pair of ordinary pliers is the perfect tool for twisting and joining the ends of two pieces of wire.

To make tight bends, curls, and spirals with the wire, it's helpful to have a pair of needle-nose pliers on hand, too. These come to a finer point that lets you get into small spaces.

WIRE SCULPTURE TECHNIQUES

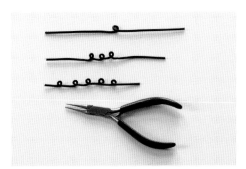
Supplies for wire sculpture

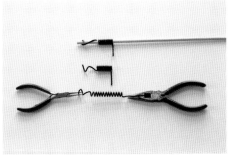
Twist wire around a skewer for a tight curl.

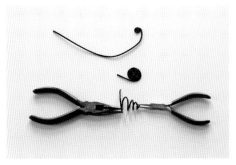
A tightly rolled spiral can be pulled out into a spring.

A simple twist can be repeated as a pattern.

Twist wire around itself to make a firm loop.

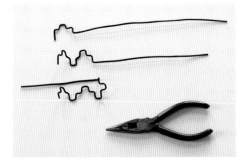
Bend right angles to make a cityscape or geometric border.

Twist two colors of wire together for variety.

Who knew you can braid wire!

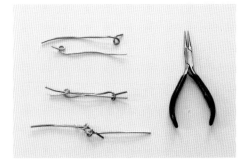
Practice knot tying techniques with two colors of wire.

After seeing a range of wire works, make something of your own out of wire.

The sculptor Alexander Calder (1898–1976) was best known for the playfulness of his work, and he used a lot of wire to make it. Calder loved tinkering with cut pieces of metal and wire and pioneered the art form of mobiles, like the one shown on this postage stamp, using wire to create true moving drawings in space.

WHAT WILL YOU CREATE?

A DANCER, A CAR, A FACE?

DRAW WITH WIRE IN SPACE!

LINES THAT AREN'T THERE

MATH + COLOR + DETAIL

Leonardo noted that just making things smaller wasn't enough to make perspective realistic in a painting—you also have to pay attention to what happens to the clarity of things as they get farther and farther away from you. "There are three branches of perspective," he wrote. The first, of course, is that things seem to become smaller the farther away they are. The second is that colors appear to fade as they recede in the distance. And the third is that things appear to lose detail as they get farther away; in other words, if there is as much detail in the background as there is in the foreground, your painting still won't look realistic, even if you get the ratios right.

Have you ever looked down a long road and noticed that things, like trees, on either side seem to magically line up and grow smaller as they head toward a point where they vanish in the distance? It happens even though you know that the trees don't really grow smaller, and they don't vanish. The trees at the end of the path are just as tall as the trees at the start.

What you're seeing is an optical phenomenon known as perspective, or linear perspective. It happens naturally when we look into the distance. An artist trying to paint a landscape or street scene or even the inside of a building has to capture the proper perspective in order for it to appear realistic.

In art, perspective means drawing or painting a subject in such a way that creates depth. This gives a drawing the illusion of three-dimensional space, guided by the geometry of converging lines. The lines (which aren't really there) meet at a point on the horizon called the *vanishing point*. When there is a single vanishing point, it's called one-point perspective.

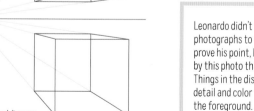

Converging lines

Vanishing point

Viewer

Leonardo didn't have photographs to work from to prove his point, but you can see by this photo that he was right: Things in the distance have less detail and color than things in the foreground.

STATE OF THE ART

Having the curious mind that he did, Leonardo was not content to simply experiment with perspective on a piece of paper. He invented his own technology, called a perspectograph, to help him study and master the skill. This machine allowed him to sketch a scene with proper linear perspective. Here is a sketch he did of a man using it. (Is it him?)

This is how it worked: He placed a clear pane of glass into a frame on an easel. Then, he looked at the glass through a narrow slot in a piece of wood, several inches away. When he was ready to work, he placed the glass and easel in front of the scene he wished to paint and looked through the slot. As he did, he sketched the outline of the scene onto the pane of glass. The outline would be his guide for the final painting and ensured that it would perfectly match the actual perspective he had viewed.

Leonardo wrote, "Perspective is nothing else than seeing a place or objects behind a plate of glass, quite transparent, on the surface of which the objects behind the glass are to be drawn."

TRY IT FOR YOURSELF

You'll need a piece of acetate to draw on, a crayon, an eye patch or bandana to cover one eye, and a window. Tape the piece of acetate to a window with a good view at eye level. Cover one eye with the patch or bandana. Stand in front of the window, several inches away, keeping as still as possible. Sketch the outlines of the view onto the acetate with the crayon.

When you're done, put the acetate drawing on a piece of white paper so that you can see the details. Notice where the horizon line and vanishing point are.

PLAY LEONARDO'S PERSPECTIVE GAME

Here is a game that Leonardo played with his friends to show them how, at a distance, things appear much smaller than they really are.

In a large room, Leonardo had his friends stand against one wall. He gave each of them a piece of straw. Leonardo stood at the opposite wall and drew a line on the wall. He asked his friends to indicate how long they thought the line was by breaking their straws to that length. Then they joined him on his side of the room and compared who came the closest. The trick, of course, was that Leonardo's line was always much longer than his friends guessed.

Try it with your own friends, but maybe tape a piece of paper to the wall before you draw on it!

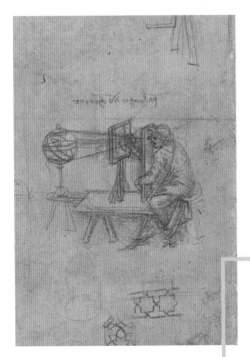

Leonardo's drawing of a man using a perspectograph, his own invention for perfecting perspective drawing.

CREATE A ONE-POINT PERSPECTIVE DRAWING OF A SQUARE

This exercise will walk you through the steps of drawing a square prism in one-point perspective. Using different colored pencils will help you see how the geometry works.

WHAT YOU WILL NEED

Sheet of drawing paper or printer paper

Colored pencils (light blue, dark blue, red, green)

Eraser

Ruler (optional)

1 Draw a straight red line across the middle of the paper. This line will be the horizon line.

2 Put a green dot somewhere on the horizon line. This will be the vanishing point.

3 Use a dark blue pencil to draw a 2" (5 cm) line that is perpendicular to and below the horizon line. Working from this line, draw a 2" × 2" (5 × 5 cm) square.

4 Use a light blue pencil to draw a line from each corner of the square to the vanishing point. These are the convergence lines. Look at the drawing. Notice you've drawn a long four-sided prism, one that goes all the back until it disappears at the vanishing point.

5 Decide how deep you want the prism to be (how far back towards the vanishing point you want it to go). Use a dark blue pencil to draw the second square. This square will be much smaller than and behind the first square.

6 Connect the corners of the first and second square, using the dark blue pencil.

7 Erase the convergence lines.

8 Use any color pencil to shade one or two sides of the prism. And you're done. You drew a box in 1-point perspective.

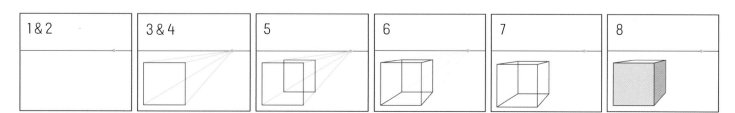

| 1 & 2 | 3 & 4 | 5 | 6 | 7 | 8 |

CREATE A ONE-POINT PERSPECTIVE DRAWING OF A ROOM

WHAT YOU WILL NEED

Drawing paper or printer paper

Scissors

Regular pencil

Colored pencils

Eraser

Ruler (optional)

Draw a room with a tiled floor.

To make a one-point perspective drawing of a room, begin by cutting the paper into an 8" × 8" (20 × 20 cm) square, then follow the step-by-step directions.

1 Lightly draw an X from corner to corner. The spot where the lines cross is the vanishing point. You will need the vanishing point the whole way through, so don't erase it.

2 Draw a 4" × 4" (10 × 10 cm) square in the center of the page. Erase the lines inside the square, all but the vanishing point. Now you have a room with three walls, a floor and a ceiling.

3 Draw a door on one of the walls. Starting from the vanishing point, draw a diagonal converging line that defines the door height. Then, draw the edges of the door.

4 Add some trim and a handle. Erase the construction lines on the back wall.

5 In the same way that you drew the door, draw a picture and frame on the opposite wall.

6 At the bottom of the page is the line where the floor begins. Divide the line into eight equal segments, making a mark every 1" (2.5 cm).

7 Starting from the vanishing point, draw lines that connect the vanishing point to the marks, extending them all the way to the front of the room (or the bottom edge of the paper).

8 Erase the construction lines on the back wall. Draw a diagonal line from the front right corner across the floor to the back left corner.

9 Add a horizontal line across the floor at the spots where the diagonal line crosses the floor lines. Erase the diagonal line.

10 Use colored pencils to add color to the tile floor and additional details to rest of the room.

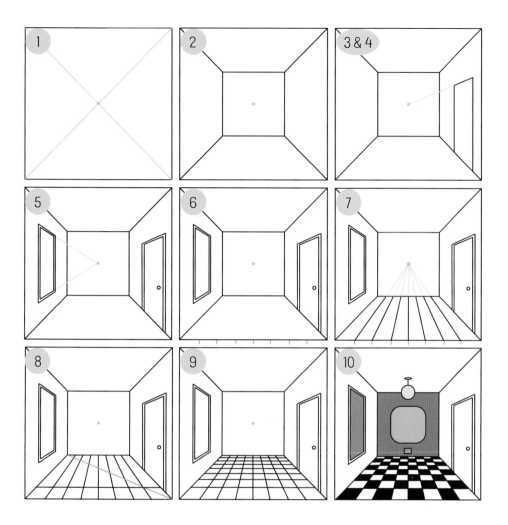

ALL KINDS OF PERSPECTIVE

One-point perspective is only one type you'll come across. Once you get comfortable doing drawings with a single vanishing point, you can try two-point perspective. Instead of approaching the subject straight on form the side, two-point perspective approaches from the corner and requires two vanishing points! But in principle, it works the same. Keep looking!

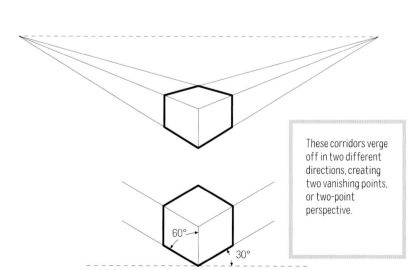

These corridors verge off in two different directions, creating two vanishing points, or two-point perspective.

LINES THAT JUMP OFF THE PAGE

This Roman mosaic from the 3rd century looks like its 3D, but it's completely flat.

This section of a church in Milan, Italy was painted by Donato Bramante to look like it's very deep, but it's only the depth of a closet.

Artists can be so sneaky. They've always been clever about using their skills to fool the eye and make you believe you're seeing something more than a flat surface. In this mosaic from ancient Rome it looks as if the white sections are three-dimensional—like little window frames that stand out from the colored interiors. But they're not. They are as smooth and flat as the rest of the mosaic. The trick is in the false shadows, created with dark gray tiles, that appear to push the white lines forward.

This section, or apse, of a church in Milan is one that Leonardo knew well. It was painted by Donato Bramante, (1444–1514), who, like Leonardo, was an inventive engineer as well as an artist. The two men were good friends and worked together on several projects. Also like Leonardo, Bramante was interested in studying perspective, and he used his painter's knowledge of perspective to create an illusion here.

The apse looks as if it has the depth of a long room, going way back in space, but in fact it's only as deep as a closet—about 3 feet (91 cm). Bramante painted it to fool the eye, using lines of convergence cleverly to create the look of a space that isn't really there.

GEOMETRY AND LINE: OPTICAL LINES

Throughout the entire history of art, artists have played with optical illusions based on perspective, but in the 1950s and 1960s, there was an exciting new type of painting that captured the modern vibe, called op art.

The name refers to the optical illusions that the paintings produce. Op art played with geometry: circles, squares, triangles, and lines. Artists manipulated the lines, bending them to create the illusion that they were lifting, swirling, shimmering, melting, or undulating like waves. The paintings might have been illusions, but the effects of dizziness they sometimes created were real.

There were no computers for artists to use in the 1950s and 1960s. They had to work out their ideas in their heads and with pencil and paper—and they made amazing discoveries, finding new ways to perceive line and geometric shapes.

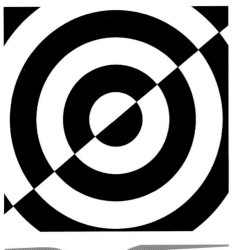

TECHNIQUES TO TRY

Some of the techniques that the artists used to create their art—and that you can experiment with in doing your own op art experiments—include:

1. Placing lines very close together so they appear to vibrate, as in the top right image.

2. Changing the direction of lines so that it appears that something is underneath, pushing the painting into shapes, as in the pink striped image.

3. Mismatching stripes, as in the black-and-white circle image. You have to blink to make the circles complete.

4. Using concentric shapes, such as the squares in the green image, but turning them askew, so that the lines of the squares appear to twist toward you.

TRY IT FOR YOURSELF

Here are a couple of exercises that will help turn you into an op artist—you can do this!

3D HAND

Trace your hand very faintly with a pencil on a piece of paper. Then, with a marker or pencil, draw parallel lines across the page. When you reach the outline of your hand, curve each line up to go over your hand, then curve it down again when you reach the other edge of your hand.

Pay special attention to your fingers and the spaces in between them. This is where the most intense 3D illusion takes place. Curve the line up and over each finger, then curve the line down in between—and watch what happens! Erase the original pencil lines and you've got your personal piece of op art. If you like, color the stripes with alternating color.

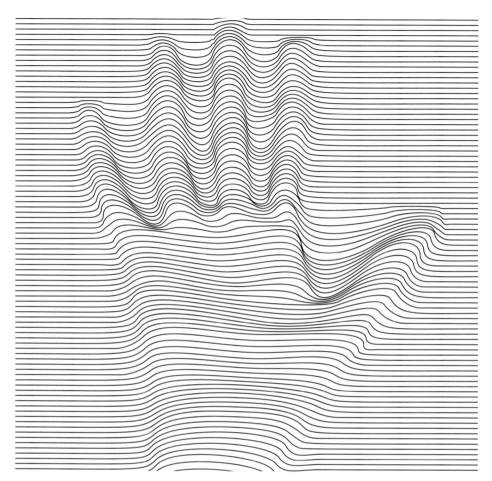

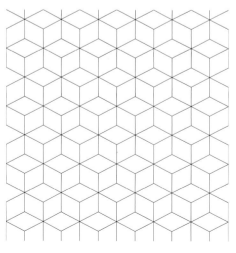

3D BLOCKS

The blocks in this design appear to be 3D because of the direction of the lines on their tops and sides. Enlarge a copy of the uncolored block grid and try it yourself. You can enhance the look by sampling different colors of stripes:

Bright colors will appear to come forward, and light or neutral colors will appear to recede. Here is a bonus optical illusion: If you squint at the striped blocks just right, they turn into a pattern of six-pointed stars.

CURVE CONSTRUCTION— WHERE ART AND MATH CONNECT

WHAT YOU WILL NEED

6 to 8 sheets of 11" × 17" (28 × 43 cm) grid paper

Pencil, pencil sharpener, and eraser (optional)

Ruler

Fine-tip markers (variety of colors)

Protractor (optional)

A parabola is a curve whose two sides are mirror images of each other. You can create parabolic curves with a 3D op art quality by using nothing but straight lines!

For this project, you'll first develop a design that you'll use as the base of your finished work of art. In order to create your masterpiece, plan to work on it in more than one sitting. Your patience will be rewarded.

PART 1:
DESIGN WARM-UPS

Parabolic warm-up: Follow these instructions to draw an L-shaped design on grid paper. Use color markers and a ruler to make the design.

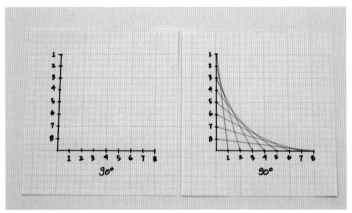

WARM-UP 1

1. Use the ruler and a marker or pencil to measure and draw a 4" × 4" (10 × 10 cm) L shape on the grid paper.

2. At the bottom of the L, working from left to right, use the ruler and pencil to measure and mark ½" (1.3 cm) increments—every two squares—numbering them all the way across to 8.

3. Do the same on the left, upright part of the L.

4. Continue to follow the diagram. Using markers and the ruler, draw a line that connects the matching numbers across the bottom and left sides of the L. Connect the 1 to the 1, the 2 to the 2, and so on.

5. Complete the design, connecting the vertical and horizontal edges of the L.

WARM-UP 2

Follow the next diagram. Try altering the angle of the L to 45°. Try altering at 135°. Notice how the angle changes the parabolic curve.

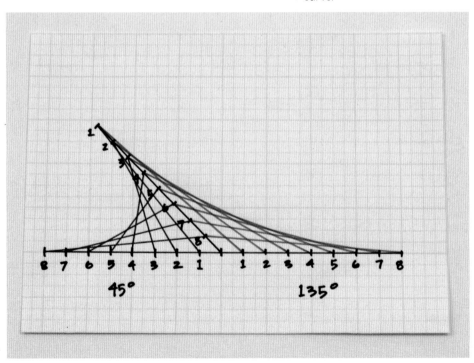

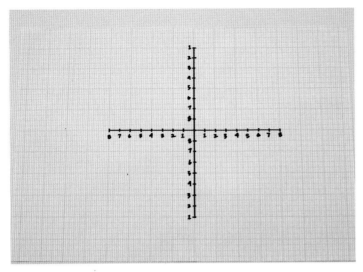

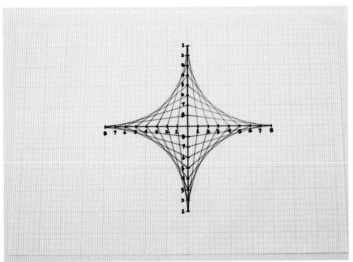

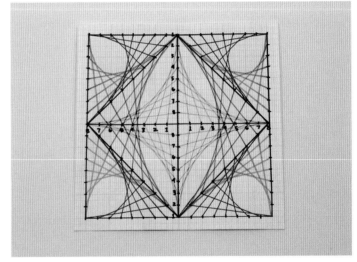

WARM-UP 3

1. Follow the next diagram. Use a marker or pencil and ruler to measure and draw a plus sign, with each line 8" (20 cm) long. The X-axis is the horizontal line and the Y-axis is the vertical line. Starting from the left of the X-axis, working from left to right, use the ruler and pencil to measure and mark ½" (1.3 cm) increments, numbering them all the way across from 8, 7, 6, 5, 4, 3, 2, 1, 0, 1, 2, 3, 4, 5, 6, 7, and 8.

2. Continue to follow the diagram. Starting at the top of the Y-axis, working from top to bottom, use the ruler and pencil to measure and mark ½" (1.3 cm) increments, numbering them all the way down from 1, 2, 3, 4, 5, 6, 7, 8, 0, 8, 7, 6, 5, 4, 3, 2, and 1.

3. Using a marker and the ruler, beginning in the upper left quadrant, draw a line that connects the matching numbers across the bottom and left sides of the L. Connect the 1 to the 1, the 2 to the 2, and so on.

4. Complete the design, connecting the vertical and horizontal edges of the L.

5. Repeat three more times, filling the remaining quadrants.

After making this 4-pointed star design, experiment with making your own designs using other number patterns.

Once you have a design that you like, save it so you can follow the next steps to make it into work of parabolic art!

MAKE YOUR DESIGN 3D

WHAT YOU WILL NEED

3/4" × 11 1/4" × 11 1/4" (1.9 × 28.5 × 28.5 cm) poplar-wood panel* (available at hardware stores)

100-grit sandpaper

Masking tape

Tack

Small craft hammer

Box of #16 × 1 1/4" (6 mm) wire nails (smooth shank)

Four different colors of embroidery floss

Scissors (a good pair)

Craft glue (optional)

*Alternative: 3/4" (1.9 cm) thick plywood (smooth surface)

TIP: If you want to paint, stain or seal your panel, do so ahead of time. Sand it, then paint, stain or seal it, and let it dry thoroughly before starting the project.

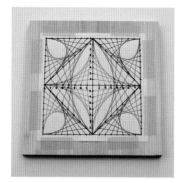

1 Center the paper with the parabolic design on the panel. Tape it in place.

2 Transfer the design to the wood panel by using a tack and the craft hammer to poke a hole into each point in your design.

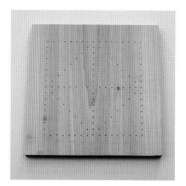

3 Carefully lift the paper to check that you marked all of the points onto the panel. Remove the paper design. Set the design at the side, saving it for steps 6 and 7.

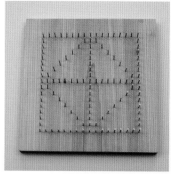

4 Gently hammer nails into the holes. Pound them in enough so they won't fall out—but not the whole way in. Leave about 1" (2.5 cm) of the nail sticking out of the panel.

5 Once finished, straighten any nails that need to be adjusted, bending them with your fingertips.

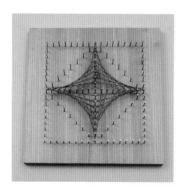

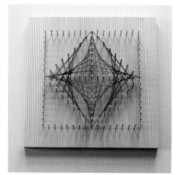

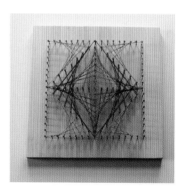

6 Select which color to start with. Begin to string the embroidery floss from nail to nail, according to your design plan, making sure the floss is taut. Tip: Tie the floss securely to the first nail. After you string the #1 nails, pull the floss across taut to the closest #2 nail, wrap it around the nail, then continue. Wind the floss around the nail head once or twice before moving to the next nail. Tie the thread off securely when you reach the end. If you think the knots might come loose, apply a dab of craft glue to the knot. Continue in this way until you have completed the design. Find a place to display your creation.

CHAPTER 4

FORMS
AND STRUCTURES

THE MATHEMATICS OF ART

In drawing the head of this child, Leonardo was clearly fascinated with the spiral forms of the curls.

Leonardo's portrait of a warrior is filled with spirals. How many can you find? Even the lion's head on the captain's breastplate has a spiral tip to its tongue.

THE ENDLESS SPIRAL

Leonardo had a lifelong fascination with patterns, and one of his favorites was the spiral. Even when it's drawn on a piece of paper, a spiral, like a spring, suggests movement and growth.

Leonardo was interested in the way that many plants branch in a spiraling pattern, that others, like ferns, grow as spirals, that seashells develop as spirals, and that human curls fall in spirals.

He referred to the spiral patterns of water and the wind as "curved motion." And he was intrigued with the whirlpools or eddies in streams—spirals that never stopped moving and yet always remained in the same place. These observations appear in his designs for an "aerial screw"—a helicopter (see page 4), with fabric-covered blades that spiral while remaining in the same place around a central pole.

ART, PROPORTION, AND RATIOS

For a painting, a building, the rooms of your house, and even the clothes you wear to be pleasing to look at and live with, the proportions have to be right—and you know when they're not. If your coat is too big, it doesn't look right. If the windows are too small for the size of a room, they don't look right. But getting proportions—or balance—right is not just about looks. It's really about getting the math right.

You've talked about ratios (comparing the size of one thing to the size of another) in math class, but artists also talk about ratios in their work. Even farther back than Leonardo's day, artists used Golden Ratio—also known as Fibonacci's Spiral—as their standard for perfection. The spiral works because, set within a rectangle made up of squares of descending size, the tightest part of the spiral's twist occurs in the smallest squares. If the twist filled the largest square, the design would appear too heavy on that side. The ratio would be off.

TWISTED MATH: THE GOLDEN RATIO

The Golden Ratio exists in nature and is related to the way things—like plants and mollusks—grow. But it took mathematicians to *understand* and write down the formula for it.

The magic of the spiral in nature is that it always conforms to these ratios, in which each new number is formed by adding the two numbers before it, starting with 1 in the center of the spiral.

The sequence looks like this:
$1 + 1 = 2$
$1 + 2 = 3$
$2 + 3 = 5$
$3 + 5 = 8$
$5 + 8 = 13$
$8 + 13 = 21$
$13 + 21 = 34$
and can go on indefinitely.

ANOTHER WAY OF PHRASING IT

Looking at the graph below, the golden ratio can be expressed this way, using division. The numerical width of the rectangle is 34.
$34 \div 21 = 1.619$

The width of the larger square is in the same (very close to the same) proportion to the width of the rectangle as the second largest square is to the first.

The same thing happens with the next smaller sets of squares: The golden ratio is a repeated pattern that works at every scale. Let's look at it in list form, starting with the next smallest rectangle:
$34 \div 21 = 1.619$
$21 \div 13 = 1.615$
$13 \div 8 = 1.625$
$8 \div 5 = 1.600$

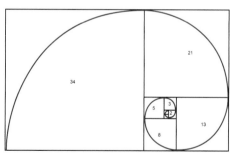

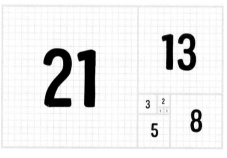

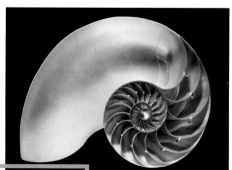

A nautilus shell.

Leonardo Pisano Fibonacci (1170–1250).

The mathematical sequences of spiral growth patterns in nature were known to scholars in the Middle East long before they were known in Europe. But in 1202, an Italian mathematician from Pisa, who had studied and traveled widely in the Middle East, published a book called *Liber Abaci* (*The Book of the Abacus*), which introduced Europeans to the math. His name was Leonardo Bonacci, and he was known as Fibonacci. His influence on Western mathematics and science was huge. Although we now associate his name with the mathematics of the spiral, he was also responsible for introducing Indian-Arabic numbering to the West, which we've used ever since: 1, 2, 3, 4, 5 instead of I, II, III, IV, V.

WRITE A FIBONACCI POEM

Use the mathematical progression of the golden ratio to write a poem. Start with one word per line and end with twenty-one. You'll know your poem is perfectly balanced because Fibonacci helped you write it. It will look something like this.

```
                    Start
                    with
                  one word
               and then add
           another—that makes two. Add
         one to two for a total of three.
     Next add two and three which takes you to five. Three and five
make eight. Go back and add five to eight for thirteen, and then eight and thirteen for a whopping twenty-one.
```

Take it further: write a "Fib" poem in which you are counting the number of syllables instead of the number of words. Fibs are a bit like haiku, with six lines and twenty syllables. Each line has the number of syllables as numbers in the Fibonacci sequence, 1, 1, 2, 3, 5, 8, and 13. Technically, the first word in the poem is a zero, so when reading the poem there's a silent pause. Like this:

```
                    You
                    too
                 can think
                 like Leo.
              Be curious and
          investigate all of the things
    around you. Wonder! Imagine! Test! Experiment!
```

PROJECT

MAKE A GOLDEN-RATIO GAUGE

Who knows when you might want to apply the golden ratio to a drawing or painting of your own? Make a golden-ratio gauge, and you'll never have to guess. You probably won't need to look too long and hard before

discovering instances where the golden ratio is waiting to be found. Use the tool to measure other objects around the house. This project requires the use of a power drill, so you'll need a little help.

WHAT YOU WILL NEED

5 jumbo craft sticks

Pencil

Ruler

Masking tape

Drill and ¼" (6 mm) bit

Eye protection (optional)

Craft saw

Miter box

100-grit sand paper

Four ¼" (6 mm)-diameter (20-gauge) × ½" (1.3 cm)-long machine screws

Four nylon washers, ¼" (6 mm) inside diameter

Four ¼" (6mm)-diameter (20-gauge) wing nuts

Screwdriver

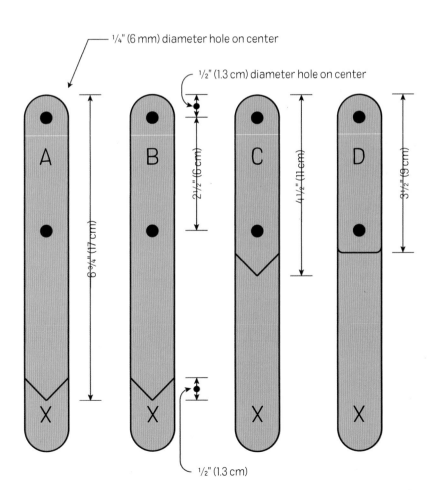

¼" (6 mm) diameter hole on center

½" (1.3 cm) diameter hole on center

6¾" (17 cm)

2½" (6 cm)

4½" (11 cm)

3½" (9 cm)

½" (1.3 cm)

A

B

C

D

X

X

X

X

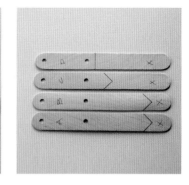

1 Use the pencil and ruler to mark the locations of the two 1/4" (6 mm) holes on one craft stick.

2 Stack the five craft sticks, placing the one with the drill hole locations on top. Tightly wrap the stack with masking tape. (The pressure of the drill bit sometimes causes the first craft stick to split. Thus, the first one protects the others from being damaged.)

3 Use the drill to make the two holes where you marked them.

4 Remove the tape and lay the sticks flat. Use the pencil and ruler to draw the cutting pattern onto each craft stick. Label the sticks, A, B, C, and D, as shown.

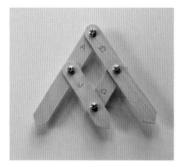

5 Use the craft saw to cut the craft sticks.

6 Use the sandpaper to lightly sand the drill holes and cuts.

7 Refer to this photograph when following steps 7, 8, 9, and 10. Attach A and B (the long craft sticks) together, as shown. Connect them using the machine screw, washer, and nut. The nylon washer goes between the two craft sticks.

8 Attach part C (the medium-length craft stick) and part A, as shown, just as you did in step 7.

9 Attach part D (the shortest craft stick) and C as shown, as before.

10 Use a screwdriver to tighten the connections. Not too tight—you need to be able to open and close the tool. Finished! Now test the tool.

TRY THIS:
FIND THE GOLDEN RATIO IN A PAIR OF INDEX CARDS.

Lay two index cards on your work surface in the form of an L. Hold the golden-ratio tool so that the outside tool pointers line up with the combined length and width of the card. *Voilà*: The golden ratio works with these two cards. Where else might you find it? It is all around and closer than you think.

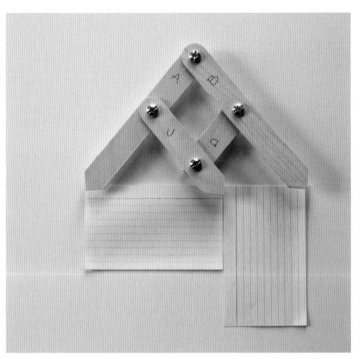

TRY THIS:
FIND THE GOLDEN RATIO IN YOUR OWN HAND.

Measure the overall distance from your wrist to your elbow. Without changing the distance of the points on the tool, move it so the tip is at your fingertip. Notice the middle of the tool points to your wrist. Try using the tool to measure other parts of your arm and hand

TRY THIS:
Use the tool to measure Leonardo's paintings and other masterworks.

THE GEOMETRY OF ART

As someone who believed that "it's all connected," Leonardo would have been delighted to discover that the geometric design he created for constructing a waterwheel was essentially the same design as the growth of flower petals.

IT'S ALL CONNECTED

As a boy, Leonardo didn't get the opportunity to study in school. His education as a young man came from his work as an artist's apprentice, so he didn't learn anything about mathematics until he was an adult. Even then, he had a difficult time with equations and square roots, but he fell head-over-heels in love with geometry. It might have begun with his studies of perspective, which, as a mathematical explanation for how we see, is itself a form of geometry.

Geometry appealed to the artist in Leonardo because it's visual—it focuses on shapes and forms, and he could apply it to his compositions in painting. But the scientist and inventor in him also loved geometry because he could use it to work out engineering and architectural problems and apply it to his studies of the human body, optics, and the way plants grow, water moves, storms form, and more.

EVERYTHING IN PROPORTION

Leonardo was familiar with the golden ratio that Fibonacci made famous, but he also looked to geometric shapes as examples of perfect proportion. He created an entire alphabet using the circle and square for a geometry book called *De Divina Proportione* (*Of Divine Proportion*) by a friend of his, the mathematician Luca Pacioli.

These letters from the book *Divina Proportione* by Luca Pacioli (circa 1445–1517) were designed by Leonardo.

Quefta letera A fi caua del tondo e del fuo quadro la gã ba da man dritta uol effer groffa dele noue partiuna de laltreza La gamba fereftra uol effer la mita de la gãba grof fa. La gamba de mezo uol effer la terza parte de la gamba groffa. La largheza de dira letera cadauna gamba per me zo de la crofiera. quella di mezo alquanto piu baffa com me uedi qui per li diametri fegnati.

Quefta letera. D. fe caua del tondo e del quadro. La gam ba derita uol effer de dentro le crofere groffa de noue par ti luna el corpo fe ingroffa cõmo deli altri tondi . La api catura defopra uol effer groffa el terzo de la gamba grof fa & quella deforto el quarto ouer terzo.

This is a portrait of Luca Pacioli that demonstrates geometry with a drawing of an equilateral triangle inside a circle.

"Without math there is no art," wrote Luca Pacioli, an influential mathematician and friend of Leonardo's. Understanding the mathematics of geometric shapes allowed artists to understand the foundations of harmonious relationships—or divine proportion— in painting and sculpture.

THE GAME OF GEOMETRY

Dozens of pages in one of Leonardo's notebooks are filled with what he called *De Ludo Geometrico* (*The Game of Geometry*). These were geometric experiments on which he spent hours, using a compass and ruler to create new geometric shapes within a circle and then to try to figure out how much of the circle's area each shape used.

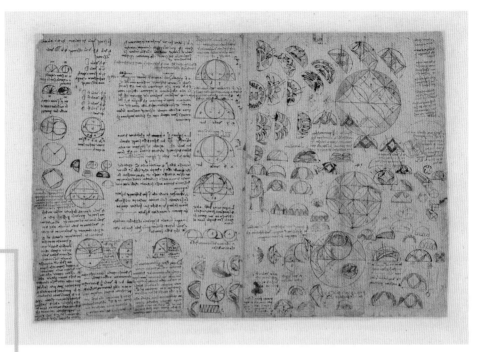

Pages from Leonardo's geometrical game.

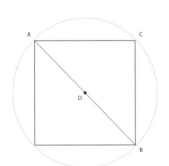

PLAY LEONARDO'S GAME OF GEOMETRY

Get out your compass, a pencil, an eraser, and a ruler, and get ready to play. See how many designs within a circle you can create. How do you get a perfect square inside a circle? Use your compass to draw a circle. The center of the circle will be marked by the compass's point. Draw a line through the center to the opposite edges of the circle. That will give you two corners of the square. Draw a line perpendicular to the first, and you'll have all four corners of the square. Draw the square, erase the interior lines, and you're good to go.

CIRCLE MATH: SQUARING THE CIRCLE WITH PI

Leonardo tried his whole life to come up with a formula for transforming a circle into a square with exactly the same area by using only a ruler and a compass. He couldn't do it because you can't determine a circle's area by geometry alone. The only way to do it is with π (pi) as part of the equation. Leonardo didn't have the mathematics training to know about using pi this way.

WHAT IS PI?

It's another ratio, and it's been known since the time of the ancient Babylonians. Pi is the ratio of the circumference of a circle to the diameter of that circle. No matter what the circle's size, this ratio will always equal pi. The value of pi is approximately 3.14. (That stays the same whether you are working in inches or metric.)

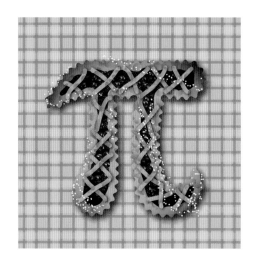

$$\text{Area} = \pi r^2 \text{ where r = the radius of the circle and pi = 3.14}$$

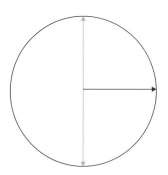

FIND THE AREA OF A CIRCLE

The formula for finding the area of a circle—any circle—is πr^2, which means "pi multiplied by the radius squared." Let's break that down.

You already know that pi is 3.14. The radius of a circle is half of the diameter. That's easy. And "squared" simply means multiplying a number by itself.

So try it. Let's say you have a circle with an 8" (20 cm) diameter. That means the radius is 4" (10 cm). To square the radius, you multiply 4 × 4 (10 × 10 cm) to get 16" (100 cm).

Now, multiply that number by 3.14.* So, 16 × 3.14 = 50.24 (or 100 × 3.14 = 314). You did it! The area of your circle is 50.24 square feet (314 sq. cm).

*You can do this on paper or by using a calculator—the calculator or an app on your phone or computer will have a π button just for this purpose.

CELEBRATE PI DAY

Now that you know the formula, celebrate π Day every year with a pizza party. When is it? March 14, of course. March is the third month, so 3.14! You choose the pie.

Note: The value of π is always given as approximately 3.14 because it actually keeps going: 3.141592653589793238462643383279502 884197169399375105820974944592307816 4062 862089986280348253421170679821480865 1328 2306647… and it doesn't stop there. It goes on forever. Much easier to multiply by 3.14!

GEOMETRIC ALPHABET

Apply design thinking and decoupage to create transparent block-style letters using only triangles, circles, and squares. Decoupage is from the French word *découper*, which means "to cut out."

WHAT YOU WILL NEED

White craft glue

Water

1 jar with screw-top lid

Measuring cup

2 to 3 sheets 8½" × 11" (21.5 × 28 cm) grid paper

Cardstock or other surface to work on

Pencil

Fine-tip colored markers or pencils

Tissue paper

Compass

Ruler

Circle and square templates (optional)

Inexpensive brush

1 In a jar, combine 3 parts of white craft glue with 1 part of water to make the glue medium. Secure the lid and shake well. Reserve for later.

2 Do some design thinking through quick sketches. Doodle ideas for geometric letters on the grid paper. Add color to the doodles using your markers or pencils.

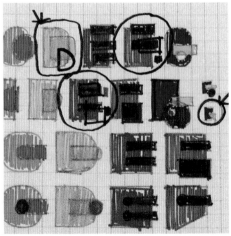

3 Think of a word or phrase you want to write in your new geometric typeface. Sketch it out on the grid paper to see how it looks, making it the same size that you want your final artwork to be.

4 Work on one letter at a time. Start with the first letter. Lay one of the colors of tissue paper on top of the final design. Gently trace the geometric shape onto the tissue paper with a pencil. Use scissors to cut out the shape. Repeat until you have all of the shapes for the first letter.

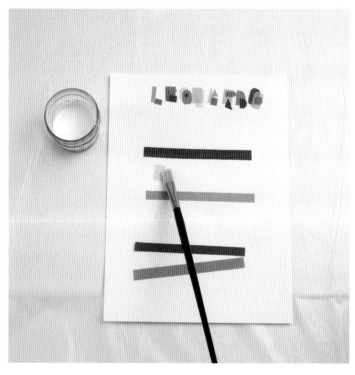

5 Paint a very thin layer of glue on the area where the first letter will go. While the glue is still moist, gently lay the tissue paper on top.

6 Move on to the second letter. Repeat steps 4 and 5 until the word or phrase is complete. Allow to dry.

7 Seal it with a few more thin coats of the glue medium, allowing it to dry between coats.

THE GEOMETRY OF ARCHITECTURE

There aren't too many geometric shapes that haven't been explored in architecture. Spheres are a little tricky, but even those have been attempted.

The homes and other buildings shown here include a mountain igloo; a thatched cottage in Ireland; plant-biome pyramids in Alberta, Canada; a Mongolian yurt; a wooden tepee; the Royal Pavilion in Brighton, England; the Loren Andrus Octagon House in Michigan, United States; and Milan Cathedral in Milan, Italy.

THE GEOMETRY

Architecture can be looked at as arrangements of geometric shapes with volume: cubes, pyramids, cones, spheres and half-spheres, cylinders, octahedrons, prisms, and orthotopes. The Irish cottage here is a box with a triangular prism on top. The yurt is a shallow cylinder with a shallow cone on top.

ORTHOTOPES?

Most geometric shapes have a single name, but the three-dimensional rectangle has several, and orthotope is one of them. Hyperrectangle and box are two more. Ortho means "straight" or "straight up"—as in orthodontist.

VOLUME MATH

Pick a building you like, decide what kind of geometric shapes it is composed of, and figure out the volume. To do that, you'll have to assign some dimensions to each part.

Let's choose the Irish cottage to start. To make it easy, we'll say that both the box shape that forms the lower part of the house and the triangular prism that forms the top of the house are each 30 feet long, 15 feet wide, and 7 feet high ($9 \times 4.5 \times 2$ meters).

Areas are measured in square feet. Volumes are measured in cubic feet. So, to find the volume of the cottage's bottom box shape, you first multiply the cottage's length by its width, which gives you the area of the base: $30 \times 15 = 450$ square feet ($9 \times 4.5 = 40.5$ sq. m). Length × width × height gives you the volume, so next, multiply that number by the height: 450 square feet × 7 square feet = 3,150 cubic feet ($40.5 \times 2 = 81$ cu. m). The bottom part of the cottage has a volume of 3,150 cubic feet (81 cubic meters).

Now, calculate the volume of the triangular prism that forms the cottage's roof section. Start with one of the triangular ends of the roof and measure the width of the triangle by the height: $15' \times 7' = 105$ square feet (4.5×2 m = 9 sq. m). That gives the area of a rectangle. To get the area of the triangle, divide that number by 2. That gives you 52.5 square feet (4.5 sq. m). Then, to get the volume, multiply that number by the length of the roof: 52.5 square feet × 30 square feet = 1,575 cubic feet. (4.5×9 sq. m = 40.5 cu. m).

Add the two measurements together, and the volume of your Irish cottage is $3,150 + 1,575 = 4,725$ cubic feet ($81 + 40.5 = 121.5$ cu. m).

Check online for the formulas for calculating the volume of other three-dimensional shapes.

FANTASY SHAPES

Architecture can be looked at as arrangements of geometric shapes with volume: One of Leonardo's pleasurable pastimes was turning two-dimensional geometric shapes into three-dimensional forms. He created a large series of fantastic three-dimensional forms for his friend Luca Pacioli's book *Of Divine Proportion*. Two of them are shown here.

If his creativity inspires you, try thinking of some fantasy shapes as architecture. Leonardo's dodecahedron on the left could make a wonderful observatory for studying the stars at night, for instance, and his rhombicuboctahedron on the right could easily be turned into a greenhouse. Try designing some fantasy architecture from fantastic shapes of your own.

Two of many drawings of 3D geometric forms by Leonardo. On the left, a duodecahedron. On the right, a rhombicuboctahedron with twenty-six open faces.

MAKE AN ICOSAHEDRON PUZZLE

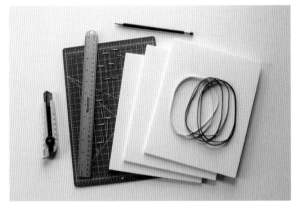

A polyhedron is a multisided geometric form (*hedron* means "seat"). In this project, you will make a twenty-sided form, called an icosahedron (*eikosi* is the Greek word for "twenty"). You'll start with 2D surfaces, intersect them to make them 3D, then join the points with rubber bands to create the illusion of sides (or seats). This takes a little time, but you don't have to do it all in one sitting.

WHAT YOU WILL NEED

Three 6" × 10" × ³/₁₆"-thick (15 × 25.5 cm × 5 mm) sheets white foam core (sold in a variety of sizes available at craft, art, and office-supply stores)

Six 7" (18 cm) rubber bands, size 117B (available at office-supply stores)

Twelve T-pins, 1½" (38 mm) long (available at art-supply stores)

Ruler

Pencil

Utility knife

Cutting mat

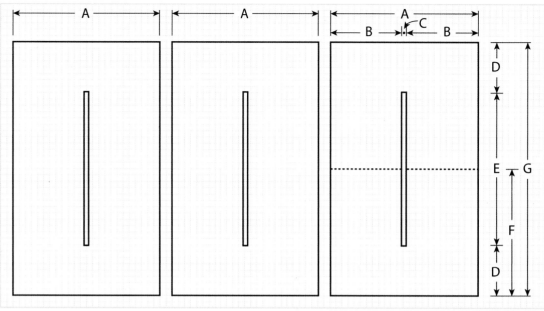

A = 6" (15 cm)
B = 2¹³/₃₂" (6 cm)
C = ³/₁₆" (5 mm)
D = 2" (5 cm)
E = 6" (15 cm)
F = 5" (12.5 cm)
G = 10" (25.5 cm)

1 Follow the diagram shown here.

2 Protect your work surface from the knife by placing the foam core on a cutting mat.

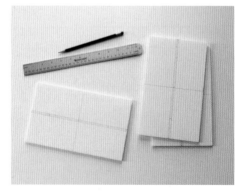

3 Use the ruler and pencil to draw the pattern onto the foam core. Precision matters, so take your time to do a neat job.

4 Use the ruler and utility knife to cut a ³/₁₆" wide × 6¹/₁₆" long (5 mm × 15 cm) slot in the center of each foam-core rectangle. Use the ruler and utility knife to cut one of the rectangles in half, making two pieces of foam core, each 6" × 5" (15 × 12.5 cm). Put these two pieces to the side.

5 Pick up the two remaining 6" × 10" (15 × 25.5 cm) rectangles. Insert the 6" (15 cm) end of one rectangle into the ³/₁₆" (5 mm) slot. Pull the board through to the midpoint. This forms the X and Y perpendicular axes of the model. Keep the model in one hand, holding it as shown.

 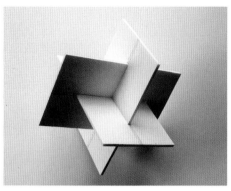 

6 Next you will add the Z-axis. With your free hand, pick up one of the small rectangles. Slide it onto the Y-axis and fit it into the slot. It will go halfway through the slot.

7 Rotate the model, then pick up the other small rectangle and repeat.

8 Push the sharp tip of a T-pin into one of the corners of the foam core. Point it toward the center axis point— the place where all three boards meet. The sharp end should not be poking out of the foam core. If it is, reposition the pin. Repeat this step eleven more times, placing a pin in every corner.

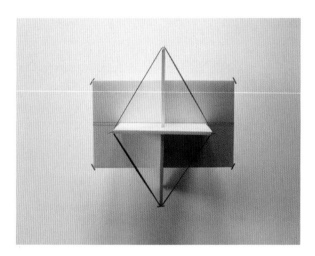 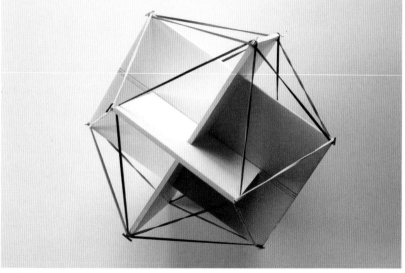

9 Repeat step 8 until the puzzle is complete.

Complete the puzzle by installing the triangular faces, which will be "drawn" with the rubber bands. Loop a rubber and over two T-pins, stretching 6" (15 cm) across the edge of one of the boards. Next, you'll need to stretch one half of the rubber band away from the edge, looping it over a neighboring T-pin as shown. The rubber band will form an equilateral triangle. Only 19 more faces to go.

PLAYING WITH FORM

WATCH WHERE YOU SIT

If you were asked, out of the blue, to draw a chair, you very well might draw one similar to the one shown below. It's a typical, everyday style that everyone would recognize as a chair.

BUT WAIT! THERE ARE A THOUSAND EXCEPTIONS!

The chair is one of the most common forms of furniture, but it's also a form that designers have enjoyed playing with endlessly ever since people stopped sitting on rocks in caves.

A chair can have legs, perch on a pedestal, or be suspended from the ceiling. It can be built of wood, molded from plastic, constructed from metal, or cut from foam. It can be upholstered, or padded, or be hard as a caveman's rock. And think of all the specialty chairs that you've seen: in barber shops and your dentist's office, in hospitals, on trains, and on space stations. A designer could spend his or her life working on nothing but chairs!

"OF EVERYTHING THAT MOVES," LEONARDO WROTE, "THE SPACE WHICH IT ACQUIRES IS AS GREAT AS THAT WHICH IT LEAVES."

The chairs shown here are wonderfully diverse, but they do have one thing in common: all of them are based on geometric shapes. As you examine them, you'll see straight and curved lines, ovals, circles, triangles, squares, and rectangles.

HAVE A SEAT

Now it's your turn. You be the designer—pretend a client has asked you to design a chair for a specific purpose. Make a list of the criteria you have to meet in order to create a successful design. Is the chair meant for dining? For comfort? For a small child? Will it be a wheelchair? A chair for working on a computer? For sitting in the backyard? Now get out your pencil, ruler, and compass and create an original chair—using only geometric shapes—to meet your client's needs.

TAKE IT FURTHER:

If you're doing this in class, try it as a design competition, with the class divided into design teams and all teams working with the same list of criteria from the same client. Give the teams a time limit and get to work! Find out who will best meet all of the client's needs.

TRANSFORMING SHAPES

Leonardo was fascinated with watching how objects could retain the same volume while transforming their shapes as they moved. He was a pioneer in the study of topology, which is the science of how objects can retain some of their properties even as they undergo transformation. Think of how water can change from a solid piece of ice to a liquid, to a gas—and then reverse and return to a liquid and a frozen state again.

"Of everything that moves," Leonardo wrote, "the space which it acquires is as great as that which it leaves." He intended to write a book entitled *Transformation—Of One Body into Another without Diminishing or Increasing the Material.*

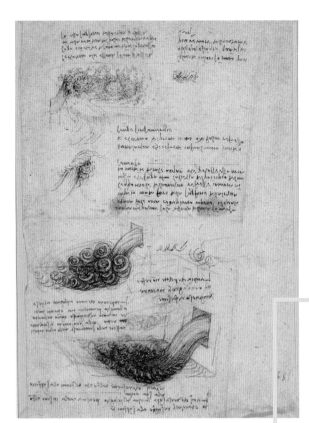

Leonardo was particularly intrigued with flowing water, watching how the water in a river could constantly change as it gushed and flowed and bounced over rocks—and yet remain the same. He did other experiments with volumes changing shape by playing with soft wax, continually reforming the same piece of wax into different geometric solids. And, as you've seen earlier in this chapter, he loved his game of creating new geometric shapes within a circle and worked at turning a circle into a square.

Leonardo never lost his fascination with the way water changes forms. These drawings in one of his notebooks show water flowing in gushing swirls.

CHANGING SHAPES

The art of origami demonstrates perfectly how something as simple as a square of paper can be transformed into three dimensions with a very different form—while still remaining a square piece of paper.

But something else happens when you reshape the paper: it becomes sturdier, harder to rip. You can use these techniques to make something structurally sound as well as decorative.

CHANGING THE STRENGTH OF PAPER

Imagine a piece of paper standing up on its edge, holding something on top of it. You know that's impossible. But you can give paper structure and strength by changing its shape.

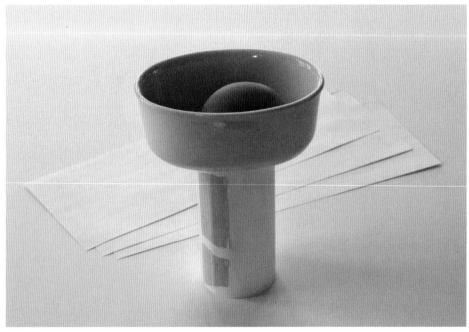

WHAT YOU WILL NEED

5 sheets 8½" × 11" (21.5 cm x 28 cm) paper

Scissors

Transparent tape

Ruler

EXERCISE: Fold two pieces of 8½" × 11" (21.5 × 28 cm) paper in half lengthwise, then use scissors to cut along the folds to make four long pieces of paper. Roll one of the pieces of paper into a cylinder about 2" (5 cm) in diameter. Tape it so it will keep its shape. Stand the cylinder on a flat surface and lay an object on top. If you use a bowl or plate, you can easily add different-shaped weights on top of the column—perhaps a hard-boiled egg or a piece of fruit. There you have it: You've made a paper column that holds weight. Hang on to it, as you will need it for what's up next.

OPERATION ACCORDION PLEATS!

Let's transform the three remaining pieces of paper by folding them into three different fold patterns.

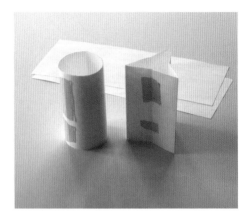

EXPERIMENT 1: Accordion-fold the paper into 1¼" (3.2 cm) folds. Curl the paper into a cylinder shape, overlapping two of the sections. Stand it up and compare it with the first cylindrical column. Without crushing the column, use your palm to apply a small amount of pressure on the top of it. Feel and see it wiggle a bit.

EXPERIMENT 2: This time, fold the paper into ¾" (2 cm) folds. Tape it into a column and compare it with the first two columns. You should be able to sense some structural differences in each column.

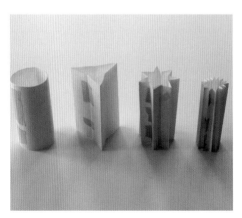

EXPERIMENT 3: Try it again with ¼" (6 mm) folds.

EXPERIMENT 4: Compare the strength of the four columns. Set them up in the order you made them. One by one, set the bowl or plate on top of the first column and add some weight. Is one column weaker than another? Which can support the most weight?

SPECTACULAR SPANS

Discover how repeated patterns of folds can make curvaceous span structures or strong faceted columns.

1 Print a copy of the two patterns at 400%. This will enlarge each pattern to 9³/₄" × 15¹/₂" (24.6 × 39 cm).

2 Cut out the patterns, trimming away the outer edge.

A

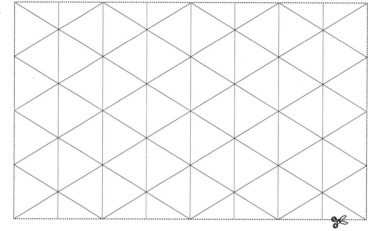

■ Valley folds   ■ Mountain folds

B

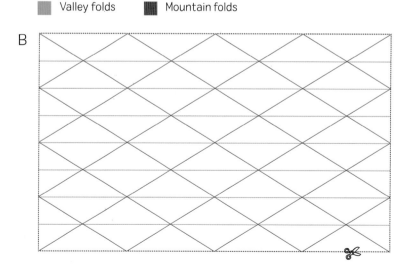

WHAT YOU WILL NEED

Access to
a color printer

Two sheets 11" × 17"
(28 × 43 cm) white
cardstock

Ruler

Craft knife

Cutting mat

Pencil

Clear tape

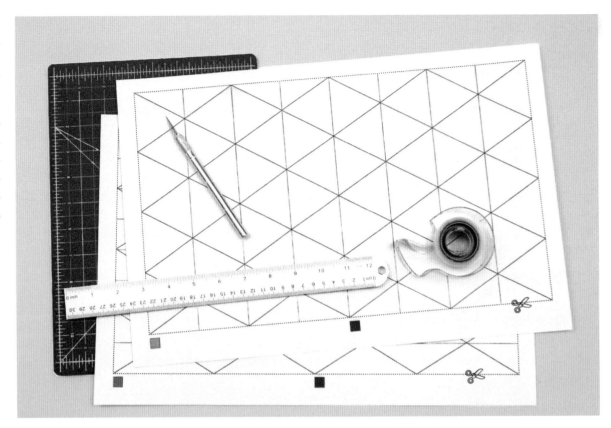

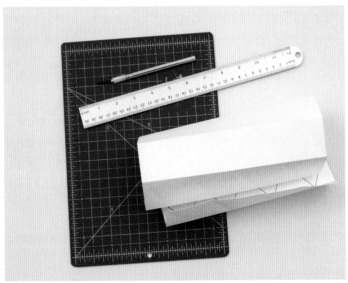

3 Place pattern A on the cutting mat so the pattern is facing up. Gently trace the tip of the dull side of the craft knife blade over the red lines (mountain folds), lightly scoring the surface. (Don't bear down hard or you'll cut through the paper!) The scores will make the mountain folds crisp.

4 Gently trace the tip of the dull side of the craft knife blade over the green lines (valley folds), lightly scoring the surface.

5 Crease the green valley folds. You are beginning to give the paper structure.

6 Crease the red mountain folds. Almost done.

7 Use your hands to coax the cardstock to make the sculptural form. *Notice how the pattern overlaps onto itself*. It will be a long column with triangular facets.

8 Tape the column at the top, middle, and bottom so it keeps its shape.

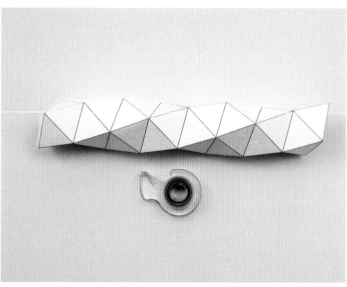

9 Make the other pattern, following the same steps 3 through 8. Tip: This pattern will fold into the desired shape more easily if you crease all of the folds extra crisply.

10 Compare the structure of the two span patterns. Notice that the crease pattern is the same, but an adjustment in the geometry results in its curvature.

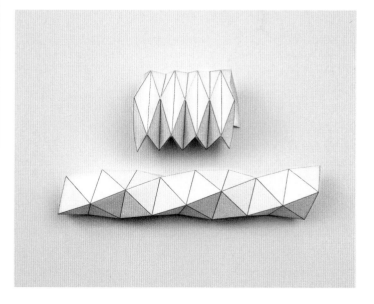

A SIMPLE PRINCIPLE

The simple act of pleating makes paper stronger so it can support more weight. That's because the pleating prevents the paper from bending or collapsing. Similarly, a folded-paper fan is strong enough to create a stiff breeze. The pleats inside corrugated cardboard make the paper surface strong enough to be used for cartons or even for cardboard furniture.

CHAPTER 5

OPTICS
AND SPECIAL EFFECTS

THE EYE
AND PERCEPTION

WHAT WE SEE AND WHAT WE THINK WE SEE

Have you ever wondered why the eyes in certain portraits seem to follow you as you move around a room? It's all in the pupils of the eyes. When you look at the *Mona Lisa*, she seems to be looking straight back at you—but when you stand directly in front of her and look closely at the pupils in her eyes, you'll see that one is looking in a slightly different direction than the other. Ergo, one of them appears to follow you whether you move to the left or the right.

Throughout his long life, Leonardo remained fascinated with his studies of optics, or how we see. He studied optics from inside the eye, as we saw in our chapter on light, and he studied optics from outside, as we saw in the chapter on color. He never stopped studying the tricks of visual perception: how the use of shadows in painting appears to make objects three dimensional, and how applying the geometry of perspective can make a flat painting appear to have the depth of infinite space.

With his love of geometric and perspective games, surely Leonardo would have enjoyed the work of another artist who came along four centuries later: M.C. Escher. If you don't know M.C. Escher by name, you might be familiar with his work anyway. The shifting staircases at Hogwarts in the Harry Potter movies were inspired by Escher's work.

Maurits Cornelis Escher (1898–1972) was a Dutch artist, draftsman, and mathematician who is renowned for creating magnificent, mesmerizing tessellations. The design shown here is inspired by Escher's work. Notice the clever way the individual shapes nest and how the use of light against dark plays with your eyes. Stare at the design—at once you see one animal, but when you blink, another becomes visible. That's the magical visual delight of tessellations.

PLAYING WITH PERCEPTION

Escher was a master at creating optically baffling drawings that appear to move forward and backward in space at the same time. He did it by creating geometrically impossible drawings such as these, which play with perspective. But he also did it through a type of drawing called tessellation. The word *tessella* means "small square," in Latin, and it originally referred to the square tiles used for creating repeat patterns in mosaics. Escher used the same technique of repeat patterns in his drawings to play games of perception.

"The things I want to express are so beautiful and pure."
—M.C. Escher

PATTERN, SYMMETRY, TESSELLATION

In both design and nature, a *pattern* is a shape, outline, or form that is arranged in an organized, repeated way.

In both design and nature, *symmetry* is regularity in a shape, outline, or form that provides balance, equilibrium, and evenness.

In both design and nature, tessellation refers to the repetition of a geometric cell or unit that forms a pattern and interlocks. You see tessellations more than you realize. Sharpen your focus—scan the world around you for shapes or forms that repeat and fill a 2D surface or 3D space without gaps or overlaps.

Start looking for patterns, symmetry, and tessellations, and suddenly you'll notice them all around. Imagine: For most of your waking life, you've been perceiving these beautiful visual phenomena without even realizing it!

Tessellation in the magnificent geometry of the honeycombs created by bees; in the intricate beauty of Islamic tilework; and in the magic of a Escher-style drawing.

PROJECT

MAKE AN ESCHER-INSPIRED DESIGN

In this project, you will design a 2D tessellation—a shape that repeats to fill a surface with no gaps and no overlapping parts allowed.

Create a primary cell to use as the beginning of your project. A cell is the basis for how a tessellated drawing is created. Begin with a square. Draw a V shape at the top edge. Remove the V shape from the top edge and place it at the bottom edge.

WHAT YOU WILL NEED

Pencil sharpener

Pencil

Eraser

Ruler

Two sheets 8½" × 11" (21.5 × 28 cm) square grid paper (¼" [6 mm] grid size)

One sheet 8½" × 11" (21.5 × 28 cm) white paper

Colored markers

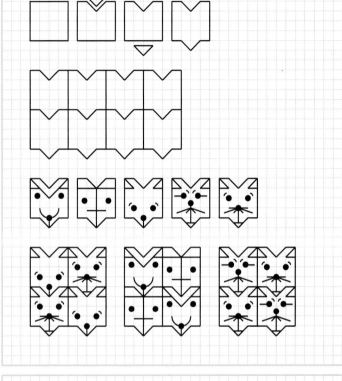

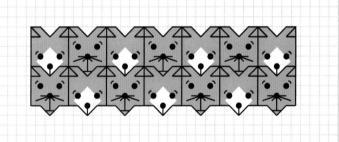

1. Use a pencil to copy the primary cell onto grid paper. Lay the grid paper on top of the outline—you should be able to see the outline through the paper. Line up the grid of the paper with the design. Trace the design.

2. Imagine the cell is a head with a face. Sketch the eyes, nose, and any other details you want.

3. Select two of the designs. Move to a clean sheet of square grid paper and alternate your designs.

4. Draw the first cell in the upper left corner of the grid paper. Add five more cells across the page.

5. Move to the next row. Draw another row of six cells below the first row. Remember: All of the cells must touch each other.

6. Make one more row of six cells. You can repeat this pattern over and over again.

7. Stop there or add contrasting color to each character using colored markers.

THE ILLUSION OF MOTION

Leonardo got plenty of movement into his drawing of a rearing horse.

How do you capture motion in a still image? Leonardo was captivated with all kinds of motion: the wind, the clouds, clockworks, waterwheels—anything that moved. He liked to buy birds at the bird market, just so he could let them go and observe their flight.

He did the same thing with animals of all kinds, keeping detailed notes on the movements of each. "The dragonfly flies with four wings," he wrote, "and when those in front are raised, those behind are lowered."

Such close observations helped him with the difficulty of figuring out how to portray motion in his paintings. "Do not repeat the same movements in the same figure," he warned, "be it limbs, hands, or fingers. Nor should the same pose be repeated in one narrative painting." In other words, if you want to get across the feeling of a very active scene, make sure every part of every person and animal in the scene is moving in a different way.

A MOMENT IN TIME

Leonardo needed a very quick eye indeed to record by sight alone how a dragonfly's wings moved in a fleeting second, or how a horse's head turned and its forelegs flailed when it reared. There was no other way for him to know those things.

It wouldn't be for another 400 years—until the 1870s—that Eadweard Muybridge, a British photographer working in the United States, was able to get around that problem through photography.

Eadweard Muybridge (1830–1904) was becoming well known for his nature photography in California in 1872, when the governor of the state, Leland Stanford, asked him to help settle a bet. Stanford believed that all four of a horse's hooves lifted off the ground at once during a gallop. His opponent said no, that at least one of a horse's hooves was always in contact with the ground. Stanford believed that photography could provide the answer.

Muybridge's initial photographs of a galloping horse seemed to prove Stanford was right, but they were not definitive. Stanford was interested, though, and through his funding, Muybridge was able to continue his photographic research until, by around 1878, he had devised a way of using multiple cameras simultaneously to capture stop-motion photographs. This time, he proved absolutely that Stanford was right. Photography allowed people to see things that moved too fast to comprehend by sight alone.

A jockey on a galloping horse, photographed by Eadweard Muybridge.

INVENTING MOVING STILL SHOTS

With his love for inventing and playing games, it's hard to imagine that Leonardo wouldn't also have loved exploring moving pictures with lenticular images.

Never heard of lenticular images? You've definitely seen them on postcards and animations—maybe you just didn't know they had a name. Lenticular images move back and forth, showing you one picture, then another, depending on where you stand when you look at them. The word means "lens-shaped," or "related to the lens of the eye," and the technology was developed in the 1920s and was used for early color movies.

You've probably noticed when you've seen lenticular postcards that they are coated with a ridged plastic. That is part of what creates the magic.

HERE'S HOW IT WORKS

Two or more images are cut into strips and then are spliced together in alternating rows to form the base. Then they are coated with a layer of plastic with rounded ridges. The width of the ridges corresponds exactly to the width of the strips underneath. So, if two images are spliced, one rounded ridge will be the width of the two spliced images.

The rest of the magic comes with the nature of light. As you already know from chapter one, light travels in straight lines, but it bends when it hits a convex surface. That's what happens with a lenticular image: Light hits the rounded ridges from either side and then bends as it reaches your eyes. So, when you move back and forth in front of the image, first you see one picture, and then you see the other.

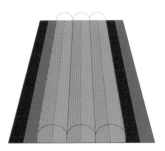

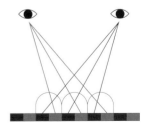

MAKE A FLIP LENTICULAR

WHAT YOU WILL NEED

Two sheets 8½" × 11" (21.5 × 28 cm) heavy white cardstock

One sheet 11" × 17" (28 × 43 cm) white cardstock

Paper

Pencil

Ruler

Triangle

Cutting mat

Craft knife

Clear tape

Colored pencils or markers

Glue stick

Left view

Front view

Right view

You can use your own motion to animate images made simply with paper. A flip lenticular is a kind of three-dimensional picture that interlaces two or more images.

This type of project works best when the two images you use relate to one another—for example, if you work with pictures of a baby's face and an old person's face, both about the same size. Or you could choose a frowning face and a smiling face. This technique can also show the passage of time if you choose images such as a tree in summer with its leaves and the same tree in the winter without its leaves.

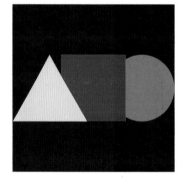

1 Use the ruler, triangle, and pencil to measure and trim the two pieces of cardstock into 8" × 8" (20 × 20 cm) squares.

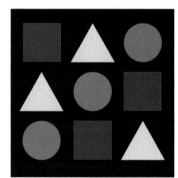

2 Create your images. Use photographs or use the colored pencils or markers to make two horizontal compositions on cardstock.

3 Lay one image face down horizontally on the cutting mat. Use the ruler and pencil to make tick marks at 1" (2.5 cm) intervals all the way across the top and bottom of the page. Use the ruler to line up the top and bottom tick marks and draw a line with the pencil. Do the same all the way across.

4 From left to right, number the strips on the back: 8, 7, 6, 5, 4, 3, 2, and 1.

5 Use the craft knife and ruler to cut the strips. Set them aside.

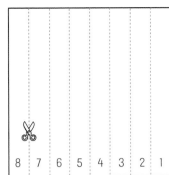

6 Repeat steps 3 through 5 with the second image, but label them H, G, F, E, D, C, B, and A.

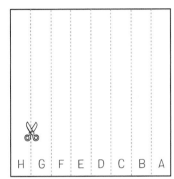

7 Set the 11" × 17" (28 × 43 cm) paper horizontally in front of you. Working from left to right, use the glue stick to attach the strips to the paper in the order A, 1, B, 2, C, 3, D, 4, E, 5, F, 6, G, 7, H, 8. Make sure the strips abut tightly, edge to edge, and are aligned straight up and down. Use the craft knife and ruler to trim away the white border. The composition will be 8" × 16" (20 × 41 cm).

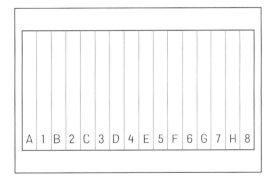

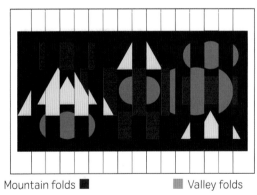

Mountain folds ■   ■ Valley folds

8 Accordion-fold the paper along the seams in the images.

9 Adjust the folds so they are all close to 90 degrees. You have made a flip lenticular! Time to test it.

10 Lay the flip lenticular on your work surface and look at it from directly above. You'll detect both of the images. To give the image motion, move your eyes right, left, right, left.

TAKE IT FURTHER:
Pin or tape the flip lenticular to a vertical surface, one you can walk past while looking at it. (A hallway is the perfect place)

ART MIRRORS LIFE
SPECULAR REFLECTION

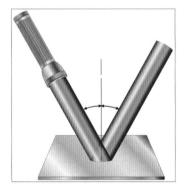

Most everything around us reflects light—if it didn't, we wouldn't see it. Surfaces, such as a white wall for instance, reflect light so well it can dazzle our eyes or light up a room.

But some surfaces have a special characteristic and reflect light in such a way that the reflection is exactly the same as the original light. This is called "specular reflection"; it's also what we call a mirror. In fact, *speculum* is an old-fashioned name for mirror.

THE GLOSSIER THE BETTER
Here is what happens. When light hits a matte white wall, it diffuses. That means that when light hits the wall at a certain angle (called the angle of incidence), the dull surface of the wall bounces the light back at us at many different angles, which is why it helps to light up a room.

But when light hits a very smooth, glossy surface in specular reflection, there is no diffusion. The angle of incidence is exactly the same as the angle of reflection. Specular reflection reflects all of the light back at the same angle—and so we see the reflection in the surface. Of course, because the reflection is coming back at us, it's reversed.

NATURAL REFLECTION
This effect happens in nature. When there is no wind, and the surface of a lake is absolutely glossy—without a ripple in sight—and the angle of sunlight is just right, you'll see a perfect mirrored reflection of the surrounding landscape. Because it's reversed, it will look like the trees are growing upside down, toward the bottom of the lake.

REFLECTIVE METALS
The people in ancient cultures, including Egypt and China, made hand mirrors from polished metals, such as bronze. As the art of glassmaking advanced, craftsmen made "looking glasses" by applying very thin sheets of polished metal to glass tiles or to thin sheets of rock crystal.

An Ancient Egyptian bronze mirror with a handle in the shape of the goddess Isis.

In Europe, a more modern process of making glass mirrors with a vapor of mercury—a (poisonous) silvery metal that is liquid at room temperature—mixed with other precious metals was developed during the Middle Ages.

THE MIRROR IN ART

People loved being able to look at themselves, but in those early days, most people did not have mirrors in their houses. Mirrors were small and very expensive, so only the wealthiest people could afford them. But artists loved them. From the Middle Ages onward, mirrors began to appear in tapestries and paintings.

Painting a portrait that included an image of a mirror in the room was a way of showing how wealthy and important the subject was. But more than that, mirrors allowed artists a touch of magic in their paintings. They allowed the artist and the viewer to see something that wasn't in front of their eyes. A mirror could allow you to see the front and the back of someone at the same time or to look into the next room—this was revolutionary in painting. It was a mix of science and sorcery!

In this scene of a money lender and his wife, painted by the Belgian artist Quentin Metsys around 1524, there is a small convex mirror on the worktable. The mirror allows the viewer to look into another room, where you can see a man reading a book and the town outside the window.

In this French tapestry from the 1400s, a woman shows a unicorn its face in a mirror. The mirror is small, but it is framed and set on a golden stand because it was valuable.

MAKE AN INFINITY SCOPE

Assemble plastic mirrors into a square or triangular prism to make an infinite space multiplier.

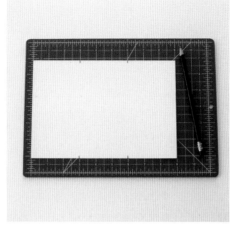

1 Lay the flexible mirror sheet face down horizontally on your work surface. Use the ruler and black marker to divide the 9" (15 cm) edge into three 3" (7.5 cm) lengths. Mark the lengths on both the top and bottom edges.

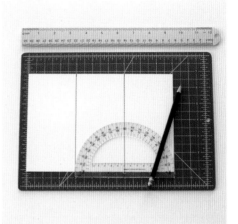

2 Use these marks to draw a vertical line every 3" (7.5 cm).

WHAT YOU WILL NEED

6" × 9" (15 × 23 cm) flexible plastic mirror sheet

Cutting mat

Fine-tip black marker

Ruler

Protractor

Utility knife

Masking tape

3 Place the mirror reflective-side down on the cutting mat. Repeat steps 1 and 2, cutting the mirror into three 3" (7.5 cm) lengths.

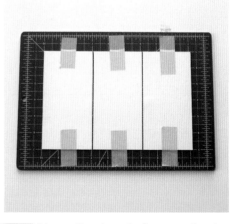

4 Line up the pieces to form a rectangle with 1/32" (1 mm) of space in between each panel. Hold the pieces in place with masking tape.

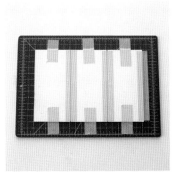

5 Tape the pieces back together along the two seams. Center a third strip of tape along the edge of the right side. Remove the short pieces of tape, freeing the mirror pieces from the work surface.

6 Flip the mirror face up and remove the protective plastic film. Avoid touching the mirrored surface; finger prints will muddy the view. (If the surface needs cleaning, wipe it gently with a soft cloth.)

7 With the mirror side up, bring up the two outside panels, positioning them to form a triangular prism shape. Join the panels by pressing the tape along the length of the seam. Get ready to try out the infinity scope!

8 Hold the scope up to one eye and shut the other eye. Look around. Move the scope, pointing it toward different things. Notice that whatever you focus the scope on becomes infinitely multiplied.

9 You'll see graphic patterns everywhere you aim your infinity scope: on a face, a feather, the surface of a leaf, tree bark, wood grain, a picture, patterns on textiles, wood grain—anything!

LOOK FOR PATTERNS!

The infinity scope is an awesome tool (and toy) for looking at images and patterns. Capture what you see in photographs and curate the images. Hold the infinity scope up to the lens of a camera and take a photo of what patterns you see.

THE EYE MIXES COLOR

"Take what nature has provided and use your imagination on it,"
Leonardo advised.

When artists paint, they take advantage of what our eyes do naturally when we look at the world around us. Colors seem to fade when we look into the distance. Two contrasting colors placed next to each other together jump out at us. Two similar colors blend together. Leonardo often created the backgrounds in his paintings in shades of blue so viewers would feel as if they were looking deep into space. His landscapes fade into mist and then into the sky. Although it's actually all on a flat surface, our eyes tell us the distance is real.

You can look at Leonardo's paintings as if you were standing face to face with the person in the portrait—you barely even see the sign of a brushstroke. The details are almost photographically realistic up close and only become less exact as they fade into the background, the way we see when we're close to a subject. But there is more than one way to see.

STEPPING BACK

After Leonardo's time, artists would experiment with a different kind of distance in their paintings so that when you step up close, the only thing you see are brushstrokes and blurred areas of color—you can't see a nose or individual strands of hair. It's not until you step back from the painting and view it at a distance that it comes into focus and the details become distinct.

Leonardo's portrait of Ginevra de' Benci is sharply in focus in the foreground and misty and blue in the background, suggesting great distance.

The farther you step back from Auguste Renoir's painting of a girl reading (1874), the more in focus she becomes.

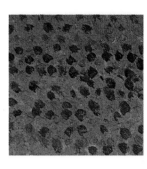

Henri Edmond Cross created his view of the sea and the shifting colors of the water entirely with dots.

Painters had long created images that were meant to be viewed at a distance, but the technique reached new levels with the Impressionists in France in the mid-1800s. The Impressionist artists largely worked outdoors rather than in studios, and they tried to capture the shifting effects of sunlight—the "impression" of how the subject appeared to the eye in a fleeting second. Scientists at that time had begun to understand that what the eye perceived and what the brain understood could be two different things. As modernists, the Impressionists pursued that idea—capturing the optical effects of light through changes in weather and atmosphere.

As accustomed as we are now to looking at the beauty of Impressionist canvases and letting our eyes bring the brushwork into focus, back then the style was too modern for most critics, who thought the paintings looked like unfinished smears. The Impressionists had to exhibit their works separately from the work of other painters.

MAKING A SCIENTIFIC POINT

By the late 1800s, artists took what the Impressionists had done one step further with a style of painting known today as pointillism. Scientists had continued to write about the effects of color and light. Most notably for artists at the time, they wrote about two principles: First was that when two colors are placed very close together, they appear to create a third color when seen from a distance. Second was the "halo effect."

TRY ON THE HALO

You may have experimented with the halo effect in science class. If not, try it now. The halo effect happens when you stare at a color and then shift your eyes to a plain white surface. Immediately, you'll see the first color's complementary color, which is its opposite on the color wheel. The reason this mattered to artists is that when complementary colors touch each other in a painting, the eye perceives a third color along the line where they touch.

Colors and their complements.

THE SCIENCE OF PAINTING

This was what the pointillists tried to capture in their paintings. It was a scientific approach to painting, placing precise dots, or points, of color next to each other, creating an optical effect—allowing the viewer to perceive a full range of colors.

The most famous of all pointillist paintings is Georges Seurat's masterwork, *A Sunday on La Grande Jatte*. It's the size of an entire wall, around 7 by 10 feet (2 × 3 m). Look at it closely: The entire canvas is painted in tiny dots in complementary colors, which your eye blends into new colors when you look at it from a distance.

It took Georges Seurat two years to paint his pointillist masterpiece, *A Sunday on La Grande Jatte* (1884-86).

PROJECT

OPTICAL COLOR MIXING

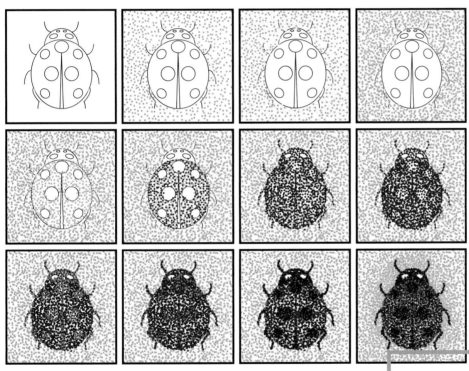

Use your mind and eyes to optically mix dots of color and make a colorful geometric composition using the pointillism technique. Include at least three geometric shapes in the composition. Start by sketching on paper, then copy your design to canvas!

Here is an example of how to make a ladybug composition out of many dots of colors. It was inspired by the work of Charley Harper (1922–2007), a modernist wildlife illustrator, graphic designer, and ecologist whose work is colorful, geometric, graphic, and whimsical.

Take a close look at this step-by-step sequence for mixing color optically, using lots of dots.

WHAT YOU WILL NEED

Grid paper

Pencil

Ruler

Colored markers

Cardstock

Eraser

Acrylic paints and brushes (optional)

1 With your pencil and ruler, divide the grid paper into workable-sized squares.

2 Make pencil sketches of your design ideas inside several squares.

3 In the adjacent squares, create the same designs, using dots instead of lines. Use colored markers to make the dots. Think about what colors you want to use for the shapes and the background. Think about design options such as overlapping shapes and variation of scale.

4 Select your favorite design and copy it, larger, onto the cardstock. You can do this lightly with pencil first and then erase the lines later.

5 Refer to the sequence of steps in the ladybug drawings on page 129 to guide you through your design, using colored markers or dots of acrylic paints.

6 Choose the main color for the background, then apply small dots of that color, leaving space around the dots.

7 Select similar (analogous) colors to stipple next to the first set of colors. If you have a green shape, add yellow, yellow-green, blue, and blue-green dots.

8 Move to objects in the foreground, starting with the main color. Continue to build the color, adding more complexity. If you have a red object, add orange, orange-red, pink, violet, and violet-red dots.

9 Sign your work with you name and date, then display it where you can enjoy it.

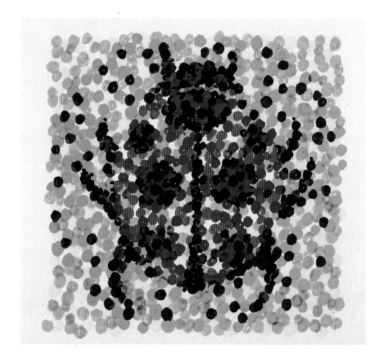

THE ESSENTIAL LEONARDO

A LITTLE ABOUT LEONARDO

MAKE A NOTEBOOK AND USE IT LIKE A GENIUS!

Leonardo doesn't say much about himself in his notebooks. Sometimes he wrote down lists of things he wanted to investigate or reminders of things to do, but he didn't leave a record of his day-to-day activities or his thoughts about personal matters.

Portraits of Leonardo always show him as an older man. This one was done by his companion Francesco Melzi around 1515—four years before Leonardo died at age sixty-seven. It's hard to tell with his long hair and beard, but according to those who knew him, Leonardo was extremely handsome as a young man.

The artist and writer Giorgio Vasari (1511–1574) wrote about every important Renaissance artist in his book *The Lives of the Most Excellent Painters, Sculptors, and Architects* and could barely contain his rapturous description of Leonardo: "occasionally, in a way that transcends nature, a single person is marvelously endowed by heaven with beauty, grace, and talent in such abundance that he leaves other men far behind... this was true of Leonardo da Vinci, an artist of outstanding physical beauty who displayed infinite grace in everything he did and who cultivated his genius so brilliantly that all problems he studied he solved with ease..." Wow.

In addition to being brilliant and beautiful, according to others who knew him, he was charming, elegant, amusing, an excellent conversationalist, and physically very strong. He loved music and could sing and play instruments, his love of nature and of animals in particular made him a lifelong vegetarian, and he was delightful to be with. He had it all.

TEACHING HIMSELF

Leonardo was aware of his lack of formal education. He had no schooling in Greek and Latin and therefore couldn't read the important works of philosophy and natural history—but he read everything he could in translation. He was aware of how specially gifted he was, but he didn't brag about it. He treasured his gifts and made the most of them, and fortunately he shared them with us in the form of his notebooks.

He wrote and drew in his notebooks daily for forty years, filling 13,000 pages jam packed with his notes and drawings of inventions, theatrical equipment, geometry games, observations on weather, notes on shadows and light, anatomical demonstrations, discussions of the circulatory system, drawings of flowers and clouds, studies of the sun and moon and the solar system, sketches of people and trees, and so much more. In Leonardo's mind, everything was connected. He never stopped teaching himself, and he never stopped learning. Only about half of Leonardo's notebook pages still exist. It's sad to think of what has been lost, but we have enough to give us a glimpse into the mind of a genius.

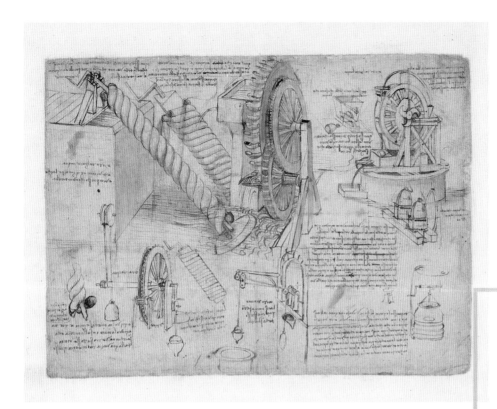

Leonardo filled this page of his notebooks with ideas for machines to lift water.

KEEP YOUR OWN NOTEBOOK

Leonardo kept a notebook with him at all times, tucked into his belt, so he could pull it out and make notes and sketches, or write down thoughts wherever he was, on the spot. Good idea. Keeping a notebook with you is a practice you might want to adopt. Keep it with you and use it. Sure, you can keep notes electronically on your phone or tablet, but it's not quite the same. It's been shown that we remember things better when we make notes by hand, and an open page allows you to combine your notes with sketches and plans that you can go back and look at later. In fact, each notebook becomes a time capsule of what you were thinking and where you went with your ideas.

Famously, Leonardo wrote backward, from right to left, in most of his notebooks. He didn't do so to be cryptic but because he was left handed and found it easier to write that way. You might try it just for fun—and if you're left handed, you might find it suits you.

On the following pages you'll find steps for making two kinds of notebooks. Make one, make a lot of them, and fill them all—don't worry if your thoughts and sketches aren't as brilliant as Leonardo's. The fun and the discovery are in the process of doing it. Leonardo never did get to experience flight as he dreamed, but he never stopped dreaming.

Make a notebook and use it—like a genius!

PROJECT

LEAN ZINE

You can make this simple book in
no time, using one piece of paper.
It'll fit in your shirt pocket for those
Leonardo moments when you need to
jot something down.

Follow the photos
shown here when
making your book
mockup.

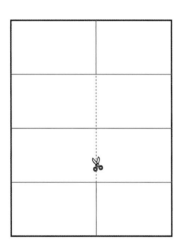

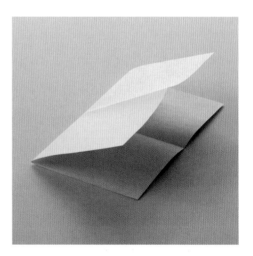

1 Fold the paper
lengthwise. Crease the
fold. Open the sheet.

2 Fold the paper in the
opposite direction,
horizontally. Crease
the fold.

3 Again, fold the paper horizontally. Crease the fold.

4 Open the last fold, and then the paper will again be folded in half. Use scissors to cut along the middle, all the way to the last fold, as shown.

5 Pinching the middle fold near the cut, pull the cut open and rotate the paper down to form four open spreads. Close the book and crease one last time.

6 Write the page numbers in the lower right corner of each page in the book, then open it up flat. Now you can see how you can lay out the pages and use a photocopier to print your book on one side of a sheet of paper.

DIY LEONARDO NOTEBOOK

Make your own custom notebook where you can record your thoughts, ideas, and observations, just like Leonardo! This simple notebook is made with binder rings so that it can lie flat or fold back and so you can easily add and subtract pages.

WHAT YOU WILL NEED

Thirty to forty sheets 8½" × 11" (21.5 × 28 cm) paper

Five sheets 8½" × 11" (21.5 × 28 cm) color cardstock

Adjustable 3-hole punch

Pencil

Ruler

Cutting mat

Craft knife

One binder clip

Three 1" (2.5 cm) binder rings (book rings)

Two 8½" × 5¼" (21.5 × 13 cm) sheets chipboard or cardboard

Triangle

1 Gather your paper and cardstock. Arrange all of the sheets in stacks of five. Choose one of the stacks, line up all the sheets neatly, and place the stack on a cutting mat.

3 Adjust the hole punch so it will punch three holes in the 8½" (21.5 cm) vertical length of the paper, as shown. Ask an adult for help. The first and third holes will be 1½" (3.81 cm) from the top and bottom of the page. Punch the holes.

2 Use the ruler and pencil to measure and mark the 5½" (13 cm) spots on both of long edges of the paper. Line up the ruler on the marks and use a craft knife to cut the stack of paper in half. Repeat with the other stacks until all of the sheets are cut. You will now have sixty to eighty sheets of paper and ten sheets of cardstock, each half the original size. Keep the paper organized in stacks of five sheets.

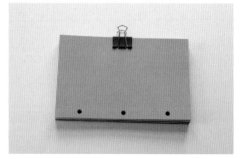

4 Divide the white paper into sections using the cardstock sheets. Hold the sheets together with the binder clip.

5 Measure, mark, and trim the chipboard or cardboard. Use the ruler and pencil to measure and draw two 8½" × 5¾" (21.5 × 14.5 cm) rectangles on the board. Use a triangle to make sure the corners are square (90 degrees). Place one of the boards on the cutting mat. Use a craft knife and ruler to trim the board to 8½" × 5¾" (21.5 × 14.5 cm). Repeat with the other board. Use a hole punch to make three holes on the vertical edge of the board. These boards will be the front and back covers.

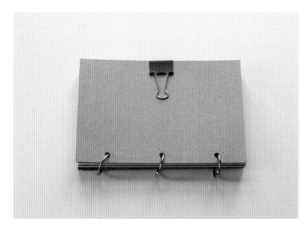

6 Lay the back cover on the work surface. Stack the sheets of paper on top, and then the front cover. Use the binder clip to hold everything in place. Guide the rings through the holes and close them tight. Customize the front and back covers with any technique you wish—drawing, stamps, block printing, embroidery, duct tape, collage, or anything else of your choice.

MAKE IT MOBILE

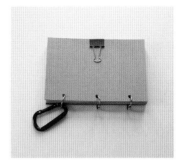

OPTION 1
Add a carabiner to one of the binder rings. Attach the book to your belt loop or backpack.

OPTION 2
Cut a 36" (91 cm) length of parachute cord and tie both ends to one or two of the binder clips, adjusting it to fit so it hangs over your shoulder.

HERE'S SOME INSPIRATION TO GET YOU WARMED UP:

Use the notebook as a way to discover the Leonardo inside of you.

Make a list of creative prompts and write them in the book. Commit to doing one drawing prompt every day.

Turn one of the sections into a special place for writing about things that make you curious. Give yourself a list of reminders of things you want to learn more about, such as codes and ciphers, candy making, vermiculture (raising worms), soldering and welding, wearable technology, hydroponics, biomimicry . . . chances are this list will contains clues about what makes you passionate.

Paste in tools that help you notice and decipher things: a tide chart, a moon-cycle calendar, a list of platonic solids, a measurement-conversion table, the golden ratio, the Fibonacci sequence, geometric formulas, time zones . . . what else?!

Reserve a section for writing "What if _____ . . . ?"

Write yourself an encouraging letter—backwards, like Leonardo.

Reserve a page for designing your creative license. This is like a driver's license, only better because it gives you permission to experiment, investigate, make mistakes, solve problems—you get the idea.

PHOTO CREDITS

BRIDGEMAN IMAGES

TABLE OF CONTENTS: A model of Leonardo's design for an aerial screw (helicopter). Private collection, Bridgeman Images. XOT366470

PAGE 6: Cecilia Gallerani, *The Lady with the Ermine*, 1496. Czartoryski Museum, Cracow, Poland / Bridgeman Images XCZ229152

PAGE 8: Pages from one of Leonardo's notebooks, he has sketched clouds, plants, a rearing horse, a man in profile, engineering ideas, and more—proof of a curious mind on a single spread of a notebook. Royal Collection Trust © Her Majesty Queen Elizabeth II, 2017 / Bridgeman Images ROC478414

PAGE 10: Leonardo recorded notes on his studies of light rays throughout his notebooks. Mondadori Portfolio, Bridgeman Images MEB 944072

PAGE 11: A replica of Newton's color wheel. Dorling Kindersley/ UIG / Bridgeman Images UIG844476

PAGE 23: Face of an angel. Detail from *Virgin of the Rocks*, 1483–1490, oil on panel transferred to canvas, 197 × 120 cm. De Agostini Picture Library. G. Dagli Orti. Bridgeman Images BL72634

PAGE 36: From one of Leonardo's notebooks: Studies of reflections from concave mirrors. On the right-hand page Leonardo details that in using concave mirrors of equal diameter, the one that has a shallower curve will concentrate the highest number of reflected rays on to a focal point, and 'as a consequence, it will kindle a fire with greater rapidity and force'. / British Library, London, UK / © British Library Board. All Rights Reserved / Bridgeman Images BL3284597

PAGE 45: First published illustration of a camera obscura observing a solar eclipse in January 1544 (woodcut) (b/w photo), Dutch School, (16th century) / Private Collection / Bridgeman Images XJF347901

PAGE 46: *Mona Lisa*, detail of her hands, c.1503–06 (oil on panel), Vinci, Leonardo da (1452–1519) / Louvre, Paris, France / Bridgeman Images XIR183793

PAGE 47: Silhouette of Sarah Faraday (1800–79) from Michael Faraday's scrapbook, 1821 (ink on paper), Faraday, Michael (1791–1867) / The Royal Institution, London, UK / Bridgeman Images TRI168546

PAGE 47: *A Sure and Convenient Machine for Drawing Silhouettes*, c.1790 (engraving), English School, (18th century) / Science Museum, London, UK / Bridgeman Images NRM260289

PAGE 51: Still from a silhouette animation film by Lotte Reiniger, 1919 (b/w photo), Reiniger, Lotte (1899-1981) / SZ Photo / Bridgeman Images SZT3050659

PAGE 52: Study of draped fabric on a Figure, c.1475–80, Leonardo da Vinci / Louvre, Paris, France / Bridgeman Images XIR181227

PAGE 53: *Portrait of Simonetta Vespucci as a Nymph*, tempera on panel, Städelsches Kunstinstitut, Frankfurt-am-Main, Germany, 1485 / Pictures from History / Bridgeman Images PFH3085720

PAGE 53: *Portrait of a Lady from the Court of Milan*, c.1490–95 (oil on panel), Louvre, Paris, France / Bridgeman Images XIR34379

PAGE 56: Reconstruction of a mechanical clock, in wood, from a design by Leonardo / Museo Leonardiano, Vinci, Italy / Bridgeman Images FAR235956

PAGE 57 (bottom): Study of light and shadow, from *Atlantic Codex* (*Codex Atlanticus*), by Leonardo da Vinci, folio 650 recto, Vinci, Leonardo da (1452–1519) / Biblioteca Ambrosiana, Milan, Italy / De Agostini Picture Library / Bridgeman Images VBA436298

PAGE 74 (bottom): Detail: Perspectograph with man examining inside from the *Atlantic Codex* (*Codex Atlanticus*) by Leonardo da Vinci, folio 5 recto / Biblioteca Ambrosiana, Milan, Italy / De Agostini Picture Library / Bridgeman Images VBA435008

PAGE 77: Cloister at Pater Noster Church and Convent, Jerusalem, Israel, 2007 (photo) / © Samuel Magal, Sites & Photos Ltd. / Bridgeman Images SAP478937

PAGE 78 (left): Roman mosaic of polychrome geometric motifs. 3rd century B.C. / Tarker / Bridgeman Images TRK1109481

PAGE 78 (right): Italy, Milan, Church of Saint Mary Staying with Saint Satyrus, High altar, by Donato Bramante / De Agostini Picture Library / G. Cigolini / Bridgeman Images DGA763233

PAGE 86 (left): Leonardo's portrait of a warrior. London, British Museum / Bridgeman Images DGA 502949

PAGE 86 (right): In drawing the heads of this child, Leonardo was clearly fascinated with the spiral forms of his curls. Musée des Beaux-Arts, Caen, France, Bridgeman Images XIR161995

PAGE 88: Leonardo Pisano Fibonacci (1170?–1250), engraving by Pelle. Bridgeman Images XRD1728573

PAGE 92 (right): Study of water wheel, from *Atlantic Codex* (*Codex Atlanticus*) by Leonardo da Vinci, folio 695 recto/ Biblioteca Ambrosiana, Milan, Italy / De Agostini Picture Library / Bridgeman Images VBA436388

PAGE 92 (left): Detail of a rose from a botanical table by Leonardo da Vinci (1452–1519), drawing 237 / De Agostini Picture Library / Bridgeman Images DGA648560

PAGE 93 (top): Letters from *Divina Proportione* by Luca Pacioli (c.1445–1517), originally pub. Venice, 1509 (litho), Private Collection / The Stapleton Collection / Bridgeman Images (A) BMR214060 (D) STC740340

PAGE 93 (bottom): Portrait of Luca Pacioli. Jacopo de' Barbai (1440/50–a.1515) / oil on panel / Museo di Capodimonte, Naples, Campania, Italy / Bridgeman Images XAL55519

PAGE 94 (top): Pages from Leonardo's geometrical game ('ludo geometrico'), from *Atlantic Codex* (*Codex Atlanticus*), / Biblioteca Ambrosiana, Milan, Italy / De Agostini Picture Library / Bridgeman Images VBA436252

PAGE 100: Drawings by Leonardo from *De divina proportione* by Luca Pacioli, / Biblioteca Ambrosiana, Milan, Italy / De Agostini Picture Library / Bridgeman Images VBA737673 VBA737675

PAGE 106 (top): Studies of flowing water, with notes (red chalk with pen & ink on paper), Vinci, Leonardo da (1452–1519) / Royal Collection Trust © Her Majesty Queen Elizabeth II, 2017 / Bridgeman Images ROC478424

PAGE 114: *Mona Lisa*, c.1503–6 (oil on panel) (detail of 3179), Vinci, Leonardo da (1452–1519) / Louvre, Paris, France / Bridgeman Images XIR291665

PAGE 118: A rearing horse, c.1503–04 (pen & ink and chalk on paper), Vinci, Leonardo da (1452–1519) / Royal Collection Trust © Her Majesty Queen Elizabeth II, 2017 / Bridgeman Images ROC399225

PAGE 123 (top): Mirror: Isis with Horus as a baby, c.1539–1295 B.C. (bronze), Egyptian School / Indianapolis Museum of Art at Newfields, USA / James V. Sweetser Fund / Bridgeman Images IMA1560632

PAGE 123 (bottom left): *The Lady and the Unicorn*: "Sight" (tapestry), French School, (15th century) / Musée National du Moyen Âge et des Thermes de Cluny, Paris / Bridgeman Images XIR172864

PAGE 123 (bottom right): *The Money Lender and his Wife*, 1514 (oil on panel), Massys or Metsys, Quentin (c.1466–1530) / Louvre, Paris, France / Bridgeman Images XIR19857

PAGE 126 (top right): *Mona Lisa*, c.1503–6 (oil on panel) (detail of 3179), / Louvre, Paris, France / Bridgeman Images XIR263527

PAGE 126 (bottom right): *Girl Reading*, 1874 (oil on canvas), Renoir, Pierre Auguste (1841–1919) / Musée d'Orsay, Paris, France / Bridgeman Images XIR33700

PAGE 127: *The Îles d'Or* (The Îles d'Hyères, Var), c.1891–92 (oil on canvas), Cross, Henri-Edmond (1856–1910) / Musée d'Orsay, Paris, France / Bridgeman Images XIR57621

PAGE 128 (bottom): *A Sunday on La Grande Jatte*, 1884–86 (oil on canvas), Seurat, Georges Pierre (1859–91) / The Art Institute of Chicago, IL, USA / Helen Birch Bartlett Memorial Collection / Bridgeman Images INC2967770

PAGE 132: A portrait of Leonardo in profile, c.1515 (red chalk), Melzi or Melzo, Francesco (1493–1570) (attr. to) / Royal Collection Trust © Her Majesty Queen Elizabeth II, 2017 / Bridgeman Images ROC399253

PAGE 133: Machines to lift water, draw water from well and bring it into houses from *Atlantic Codex* (*Codex Atlanticus*) by Leonardo da Vinci, folio 26 verso, Vinci, Leonardo da (1452–1519) / Biblioteca Ambrosiana, Milan, Italy / De Agostini Picture Library / Bridgeman Images VBA435051

SHUTTERSTOCK

Images found on pages 7, 11 (top), 16–18, 22, 23 (bottom), 24, 28–29, 32, 40–42, 46 (right), 47 (left), 48 (left), 53 (right), 57 (top row), 58–59, 62–64, 68–70, 72, 73 (photos), 74 (top), 79–80, 87 (photos), 94 (bottom right), 95 (top), 98–99, 104–105, 106 (bottom), 107 (left), 112, 115–116, 119 (top), 122, 126 (left), 128 (top)

RESOURCES

TEXTS CONSULTED FOR THIS BOOK

Learning from Leonardo
Fritjof Capra
Berrett-Koehler Publishers, 2013

The Science of Leonardo
Fritjof Capra
Doubleday, 2007

Leonardo da Vinci
Walter Isaacson
Simon and Schuster, 2017

Leonardo da Vinci
Kenneth Clark
First printed: Cambridge University Press 1939
Penguin Books, 1993

A Treatise on Painting
Leonardo da Vinci
Translator, John Francis Rigaud
Printed for J. Taylor, the Architectural
Library, London, 1802
Available as a Project Gutenberg ebook, 2014

ONLINE RESOURCES

American Museum of Natural History
www.amnh.org

Ask Nature, asknature.org

Buckminster Fuller Institute, www.bfi.org

Children's Museum of Indianapolis,
www.childrensmuseum.org

Cooper Hewitt Smithsonian Design Museum
www.cooperhewitt.org

Crystal Bridges of American Art
crystalbridges.org

Exploratorium: The Museum of Science,
Art, and Human Perception
www.exploratorium.edu

Harvard Museum of Natural History
hmnh.harvard.edu/home

The Henry Ford, www.thehenryford.org

Khan Academy, www.khanacademy.org

Leonardo da Vinci Museum,
www.museumsinflorence.com/musei/
Leonardo-museum.html

Lemelson Center for the Study of Invention
and Innovation, invention.si.edu

Maker Faire, makerfaire.com

Make Magazine, makezine.com

Mensa for Kids, www.mensaforkids.org

Metropolitan Museum of Art (MET)
www.metmuseum.org

MIT Museum, mitmuseum.mit.edu

Munsell Color, munsell.com

Museum of Modern Art (MoMA)
www.moma.org

Museum of Science, www.mos.org

Museum of Science and Industry, Chicago
www.msichicago.org

MOMATH National Museum of Mathematics
momath.org

NASA for Students Grades 5–8
www.nasa.gov/audience/forstudents/5-8/
index.html

National Museum of the American Indian
www.nmai.si.edu

NYSCI Design Make Play, nysci.org

PBSkids, pbskids.org

Peabody Essex Museum, www.pem.org

Science Channel, www.sciencechannel.com

Smithsonian Museums, www.si.edu/museums

USPTO Kids (United States Patent
and Trademark Office)
www.uspto.gov/kids/index.html

Wolfram Mathworld
mathworld.wolfram.com

World Clock
www.timeanddate.com/worldclock/

World Weather
www.worldweather.org/en/home.html

ACKNOWLEDGMENTS

Hardly any project gets done without support, mentorship, and collaboration. This book would not have been possible without the support of my family, the mentorship of editor Judith Cressy, and the professional contributions of project editor Meredith Quinn, art director Marissa Giambrone, and models Anindita Agarwal, Akhere Edoro, Jacqueline Edoro, Odion Edoro, Pascal Holler, and Raja MacNeal. Thank you to contributing photographer Glenn Scott and to Paul Burgess at Burge Agency for the book design and layout.

ABOUT THE AUTHOR

Amy Leidtke is a multidisciplinary artist, industrial designer, and adjunct professor at Rhode Island School of Design (RISD). She is a lifelong learner and educator who is curious about the way things work. She lives with her family in Rhode Island.

INDEX

A

The Adventures of Prince Achmet (Reiniger), 51
"Aerial screw," 86
Allum, for food-based dyes, 26
Alphabet, geometric, 96–97
Angle of incidence, 122
Animation, silhouette, 51
Anthocyanins, 24
Architecture, geometry and, 98–103

B

Black
    chiaroscuro drawing and, 53
    as a color, 11
    cultural meaning of, 35
    silhouette portraits and, 47
Blind contour drawing, 69
Blue, cultural meaning of, 34
Botticelli, Sandro, 53
Bramante, Donato, 78
Bubbles, rainbow colors on, 18
Burnt charcoal, ink made from, 67

C

Calder, Alexander, 72
Camera
    experimenting with shadows using, 47
    "eye" of the, 41
Camera obscura, 42–45
Carotenoids, 24
Chairs, 104–105
Chiaroscuro drawing, 52–53
Circle, finding the area of a, 95
Clark, Kenneth, 8
Clocks, 56
Color(s)
    blending together of similar, 126
    color wheel project, 12–15
    dyes and paints created from food project, 24–27
    harnessing a rainbow project, 19–21
    laying down thin layers of, 22
    making colorful shadows project, 30–31
    mixing colors of light, 28–29
    rainbow science, 16–18
    reflected, 28
    the science of, 10–11
    sunlight and, 11
    transparent, 22–23
    visual language of, 32–35
Color-light mixing, 28–29
Color pigments, 23
Color spectrum, 11, 18
Color wheels, 11, 12–15
Columns, paper, 107–111
Compass, 59, 60
Computers, mixing colors of light and, 29
Concave lenses, 37
Continuous-line contour drawing, 69
Contour drawing, 68–69
Contour use of lines, 63
Convex lenses, 37
Cornea, 40
Craft wire, 70
Cross contour use of lines, 63
Culture, interpretation of colors and, 33, 34–35

D

Da Vinci, Leonardo
    apprenticeship for Verrocchio, 6–7, 37
    birth/parents, 6
    chiaroscuro shading used by, 52–53
    curiosity and study by, 7–8
    distance/background in paintings of, 126
    drawings/sketches by, 8, 37, 52, 57, 68, 74, 86, 92, 100, 106, 133
    on geometry, 92
    on light, 37
    notebooks of, 10, 132–133
    oil paints and, 22
    on optics, 114
    paintings by, 23, 46, 53, 126
    personal characteristics of, 132
    perspective and, 73–74
    portraits of, 132
    on shadows, 46
    on spiral patterns, 86
De'Barbari, Jacopo, 93
Decoupage, 96–97
De Ludo Geometrico (The Game of Geometry) (da Vinci), 94
Designing a chair, 105
Dispersion, 16
Distance, in paintings, 126–127
Divina Proportione (Pacioli), 93
Dotted use of lines, 63
Double rainbow, 18
Drawing(s). See also Da Vinci, Leonardo, drawings/sketches of
    all-white still life project, 54–55
    chiaroscuro, 52–53
    contour, 68–69
    one-point perspective drawings, 75–77
    perspective and, 73
    tessellation, 115
    with your handmade drawing tools, 67
Duodecahedron, 100

E

Earth, axis of, 58
Egg tempera, 22
Endless spiral, the, 86
Escher, Mauritus Cornelis (M.C.), 114–115
Expressive use of lines, 63
Eye, the
    light and the human, 40–41
    perception and, 114–115, 118–119

F

Fantasy shapes, 100
Faraday, Michael, 47
Faraday, Sarah, 47
Fibonacci, Leonardo Pisano, 88
Fibonacci's Spiral, 87
"Fib" poem, 88
Five O'Clock shadow, 56–57
Florence, Italy, 7
Food-based dyes, 24–27
Forms
    chairs, 104–105
    changing the strength of paper project, 107–108
    da Vinci's use of geometry, 92–93
    geometric alphabet project, 96–97
    geometric shapes in architecture, 98–99
    the Golden Ratio, 87–88
    Golden-Ratio gauge project, 89–91
    Icosahedron puzzle project, 101–103
    Leonardo's Game of Geometry, 94
    proportion, 87, 93
    ratios, 87
    spectacular spans project, 109–111
    spiral patterns, 86
    squaring the circle with pi, 95
    transforming shapes, 105–106
    two-dimensional shapes turned into three-dimensional, 100

G

Gallerani, Cecilia, 6
Games
    Leonardo's game of geometry, 94
    perspective, 74
Geology, 7

Geometry
    in architecture, 98–99
    chairs, 104–105
    da Vinci on, 92
    fantasy shapes, 100
    Icosaehedron puzzle project, 101–103
    Leonardo's game of, 94
    prisms, 16
    proportion, 93
    tessellation and, 115–116
Gestural use of lines, 63
The Golden Ratio, 87–88, 93
Golden-Ratio gauge, 89–91
Green, cultural meaning of, 34

H

Halo effect, 128
Harper, Charley, 129
Horizontal line, 62

I

Icosahedron puzzle, 101–103
Implied line, 62, 63
Impressionists, 127
Indian-Arabic numbering, 88
Informational use of lines, 63
Ink, making your own, 67
Invisible light, 11
Iris, 40

K

Klee, Paul, 62

L

Lady from the Court of Milan (da Vinci), 53
The Lady with the Ermine (da Vinci), 6
Latitude, 59
Lean zine, 134–135
Lens (eye), 40
Lenticular images, 119, 120–121
Liber Abaci (The Book of the Abacus) (Bonacci/Fibonacci), 88

Light. See also Shadows
    bending, 37
    camera obscura project, 42–45
    chiaroscuro drawing, 52–53
    da Vinci's study of, 37
    experiment with bending, 38–39
    and the eye, 40–41
    lenticular images and, 119
    specular reflection and, 122
    straight line of travel, 37
Light, mixing colors of, 28–29
Light waves, 11
Linear perspective, 73
Lines
    contour drawing in space project, 70–72
    contour drawing using, 68–69
    curve construction project, 81–84
    fifteen ways to use, 63
    making and drawing with handmade drawing tools project, 65–67
    meaningful, 64
    one-point perspective drawing projects, 75–77
    op art and, 79
    optical illusions and, 78–80
    perspective and, 73–74
    used descriptively in language, 62, 63
The Lives of the Most Excellent Painters, Sculptors, and Architects (Vasari), 132
Loren Andrus Octagon House, Michigan, 98, 99

M

Manet, Édouard, 126
Mathematics. See also Geometry
    of art, 86–88

celebration of Pi Day, 95
curve construction project, 81–84
finding the area of a circle, 95
The Golden Ratio/Fibonacci's Spiral, 87–88
Golden-Ratio gauge project, 89–91
rainbows, 17
ratios, 87
squaring the circle with pi, 95
volume math, 99
Mechanical clocks, 56
Mechanical use of lines, 63
Metsys, Quentin, 123
Milan Cathedral, Milan, Italy, 98, 99
Mirrors, 37, 38, 122–123
Mobiles, 72
Mona Lisa (da Vinci), 114
Moonbows, 17
Motion
    portrayed with still images, 118–119
    use of lines indicating, 63
Mural from the Temple of Longing Thither (Klee), 62
Muybridge, Eadweard, 118, 119

N

Nanometers, 11, 18
Newton, Sir Isaac, 10, 11
Notebooks, 133–137

O

Of Divine Proportion (Pacioli), 100
Oil paints, 22
One-point perspective drawing, 73, 75–77
Op art, 79
Ophthalmologist, 41
Optical illusions, 41, 78–80
Optical lines, 79
Optician, 41
Optic nerve, 40, 41

Optics, 16
    capturing motion in still images, 118–119
    da Vinci's study of, 114
    distance in paintings, 126–127
    Escher-inspired design project, 117
    eye and perception, 114–116, 118
    eye mixing colors, 126
    flip lenticular project, 120–121
    halo effect, 128
    infinity scope project, 124–125
    meaning of, 41
    mirrors, 122–123
    optical color mixing project, 129–130
    pointillism, 127–128
Orange, cultural meaning of, 35
Orthotope, 98

P

Pacioli, Luca, 85, 93, 100
Paper, changing the strength of, 107–108
Parabola, 81–84
Pattern(s)
    definition, 116
    repeat, tessellations and, 115
    spectacular spans project, 109–111
    spiral, 86
    use of lines for, 63
Perception, 114–115, 118–119
Perspective, 7, 73–77
Perspectograph, 74
Photography, 118, 119
Physics, 7
Pi Day, 95
Pigments, color, 23
Pi, squaring the circle with, 95
Pleating, 111
Poem, Fibonacci, 88
Pointillism/pointillists, 127–128
Primary colors, 28, 29
Prisms, 11, 16, 18, 19–21

Projects
    all-white still life drawing (light and shadows), 54–55
    bending light (light and shadows), 38–39
    camera obscura (light and shadows), 42–45
    changing the strength of paper (form), 107–108
    color wheel (color), 12–15
    contour drawing in space (lines), 70–72
    curve construction (lines), 81–84
    DIY Leonardo notebook, 136–137
    dyes and paints created from food (color), 24–27
    Escher-inspired design (optics), 117
    flip lenticular (optics), 120–121
    geometric alphabet (forms), 96–97
    Golden-Ration gauge (forms), 89–91
    harnessing a rainbow (color), 19–21
    icosahedron puzzle (form), 101–103
    infinity scope, 124–125 (optics)
    lean zine, 134–135
    making drawing tools and drawing with them (lines), 65–67
    mixing different colors of light (color), 30–31
    one-point perspective drawings (line), 75–77
    optical color mixing (optics), 129–130
    repeated patterns/folds creating span structures, 109–111
    shadow puppets (light and shadows), 48–51
    sundials (light and shadows), 58–60

Proportion, 87, 93
Puppets, shadow, 48–51
Purple, cultural meaning of, 35

R
Rainbows, 16–21
Ratios, 87, 95. *See also* The Golden Ratio
Red, cultural meaning of, 34
Reflected color, 28
Reflected light, 29, 37, 39
Refraction, 10, 16
Reiniger, Charlotte "Lotte," 51
Renaissance, the, 7
Renoir, Auguste, 127
Retina, 40
Royal Pavilion, Brighton, England, 98, 99

S
Science, technology, engineering, art, and mathematics (STEAM), 8
Sculptural techniques, wire, 71–72
Seurat, Georges, 128
Shadow portraits, 46, 47
Shadows
    all-white still life drawing project, 54–55
    chiaroscuro drawing, 52–53
    da Vinci on, 46
    definition, 47
    mixing colors of light to make colorful, 30–31
    shadow puppets project, 48–51
    silhouettes, 46, 47
    sundial project, 58–60
    telling time with, 56–57
Silhouette animation, 51
Silhouettes, 46, 47, 51
Specular reflection, 122
Spiral forms, 86, 87–88
Spiral line, 63
Square prism, 16, 75
Stanford, Leland, 119
Still life drawing, all-white, 54–55

Stop-frame motion, 119
Structural use of lines, 63
A Sunday on La Grande Jotte (Seurat), 128
Sundials, 58–60
Symmetry, 116

T
Tessellations, 115–116, 117
Texture, use of lines for, 63
"The glory," 17
3D blocks, 80
Topology, 105
Transparent color, 22–23
Triangular prisms, 16

V
Value, use of lines for, 63
Vanishing point, 73, 75, 76, 77
Vasari, Giorgio, 132
Verrocchio, Andrea del, 6–7
Vespucci, Simonetta, 53
Vinci, Italy, 6, 7
Virgin of the Rocks (da Vinci), 23
Visible light, 11
Visible spectrum, 11
Visual perception, 114–115
Volume math, 99

W
Water, transforming shapes in, 105–106
Wavelengths, color and, 11, 16, 18, 28
Wavy lines, 63
Weather, 7, 64
White
    chiaroscuro drawing and, 53
    as a color, 11
    cultural meaning of, 35
    silhouette portraits and, 47
White light, 11
Wire, drawing/writing with lines in space using, 70–72

Y
Yellow, cultural meaning of, 34

Z
Zigzag lines, 63